NASCAR SUPERSTARS

First published in 2002. This revised and updated edition published in 2005

10 9 8 7 6 5 4 3 2 1

ISBN 1 86200 204 5

Project Editor: Luke Friend
Project Art Direction: Jim Lockwood
Production: Sarah Corteel & Lisa French
Picture Research: Debora Fioravanti & Tom Wright
Design: Brian Flynn & Zoe Dissell

Printed in Dubai

This is not an officially licensed publication of NASCAR

STATISTICS
Please note that 2004 earnings totals and career totals do not reflect bonus money from the 2004 points fund.

NASCARSUPERSTARS

Reid Spencer

SEVENOAKS

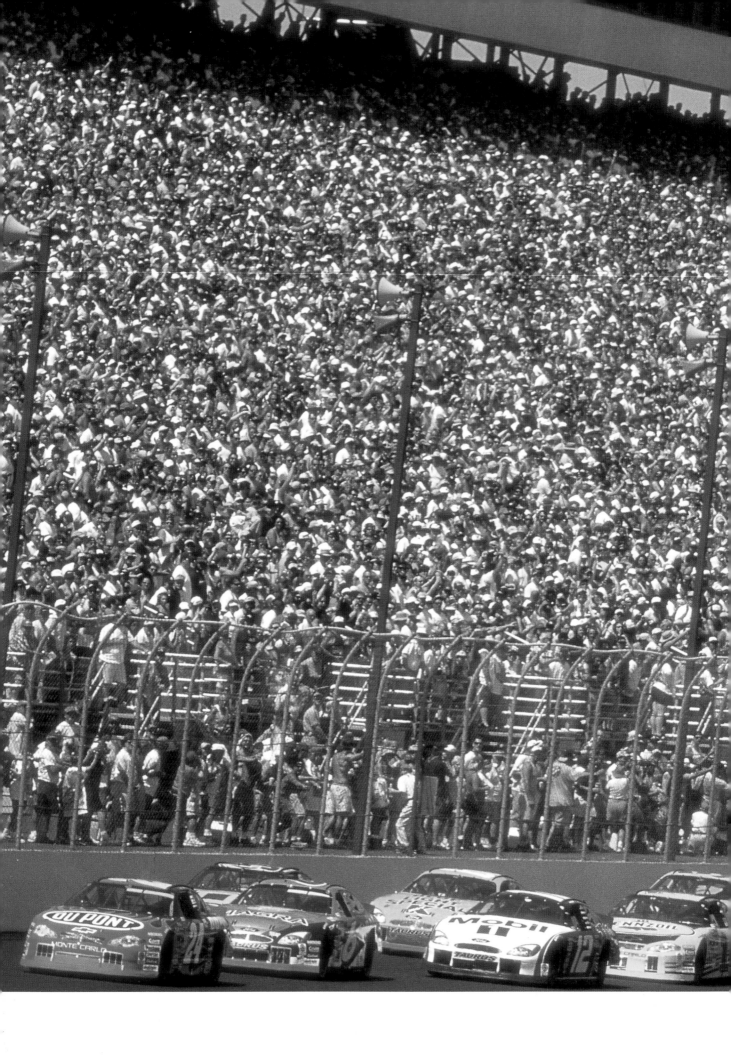

CONTENTS

INTRODUCTION

The face of stock car racing is changing, as NASCAR's elite division—the

NEXTEL Cup Series—begins its high-speed journey through the 21st century.

Long gone are the days when drivers clad in blue jeans and T-shirts manhandled cars with familiar names like Chevrolet, Oldsmobile, Ford, Mercury, Cadillac and Lincoln—along with such obsolete classics as Nash, Studebaker, Kaiser and the redoubtable Hudson Hornet—around Daytona's 4.15-mile Beach and Road Course.

Likewise relegated to the past are shoestring budgets and pit crews made up of family and friends. NASCAR today is high-tech and high-dollar. Corporate sponsors are willing to spend in excess of $15 million annually to have their logos painted on the hoods of the top drivers' cars.

No event on the Winston Cup schedule is more exciting than a night race at Bristol, one of the few traditional "short tracks" remaining on the circuit.

make from another, save for the nameplate and a few technical specifications not readily discernible to the eye—the height and width of the rear spoiler, or the length of the front air dam, for example.

Stock car racing has evolved from a regional sport indigenous to the southeast United States to a burgeoning national phenomenon. Thanks to an unprecedented growth of its fan base and a building boom during the last decade of the 20th century, "superspeedways" now dot the landscape in such diverse locales as Fort Worth, Texas; Kansas City, Missouri; Chicago, Illinois; Las Vegas, Nevada; and Fontana, California.

To the chagrin of traditionalists in the Bible Belt, these new monolithic rings of asphalt have begun to supplant the "short tracks" that were once the staple of stock car racing, but the influx of corporate dollars—not to mention a recent lucrative contract for the rights to televise the NEXTEL Cup Series—demands a national presence and a corresponding foray into larger markets.

If the face of stock car racing is changing, so are the faces of its drivers. First and foremost, the composite NEXTEL Cup driver of today is younger than his counterpart of a few years ago. The skill set, too, is radically different. No longer are daring and driving ability enough to carry the day. In a sport where the difference between winning and losing is measured in hundredths, or even thousandths, of a second, today's driver must be able to interpret changing track conditions and the subtle handling characteristics of his car and communicate them clearly to a crew chief whose function is to make critical, though often minute, adjustments throughout the course of a race.

Off the track, today's driver must be a communicator too—to potential consumers of his sponsor's product. The modern-era NASCAR superstar combines the highest level of performance with an ample dose of personal magnetism.

This book, then, is about the magnificent men who pilot the breathtaking machines of NEXTEL Cup racing.

Those corporate dollars pay for wind tunnel testing; in-house engine shops that include the most sophisticated instrumentation available to the automotive industry; pit crews trained to change four tires and refuel a car in less than 15 seconds; and in the case of the most affluent teams, a support staff of 40 persons or more, ranging from the fabricators who construct the cars to the camp followers who handle the public relations machinery for their drivers.

No longer is there much that is "stock" about a stock car. Long gone are the days when drivers would tape up the headlights of their street cars and race them on a track, be it dirt or asphalt. The modern machines are sleek and aerodynamic, with engines capable of generating more than 750 horsepower. There is little to differentiate one

The HISTORY

Before Big Bill France's vision of a national sanctioning body became reality, stock car racing was a hit-or-miss proposition, to put it kindly.

Rooted in the southeast region of the United States, the racing of stock cars can trace its origins—at least in part—to the manufacture and transport of illegal whiskey, otherwise known as "moonshine," throughout the backwoods of the south.

Outrunning government agents, known locally as "revenuers," required rather substantial modifications to existing street cars, especially where a full load of contraband was involved. Horsepower needed a significant boost, and stiffer springs were required to support the additional weight of the booze.

Racing the mechanically enhanced cars on short "bullrings" made of packed dirt evolved into a popular pastime. The growing sport, however, had no national governing body, no standardized set of rules, and no assurance that a track owner or promoter would be willing and able to pay the competitors at the end of the day.

Bill France sought to change all that and laid out his plan at a historic meeting at the Streamline Hotel in Daytona Beach on December 14, 1947. Two months later, the National Association for Stock Car Auto Racing was born, with France as its president.

Along with standardized rules, a points fund and a bona fide national championship came the iron-fisted rule of France. If NASCAR can be characterized as autocratic in its dealings with track owners and drivers—particularly in the early days—it is also necessary to understand that the sanctioning body was fighting for its life, and continued to do so in the face of challenges from rival organizations and the union movement.

The first race in NASCAR's "Strictly Stock" division, the entity that would eventually become the Winston Cup Series, took place on June 19, 1949 at Charlotte Speedway—not the 1.5-mile masterpiece that today dominates

Highway 29 in Harrisburg, North Carolina, but a three-quarter-mile dirt oval on the outskirts of town.

The first Strictly Stock race produced the series' first disqualification. Glen Dunnaway was stripped of the victory when post-race inspection uncovered illegal springs on his 1947 Ford. Jim Roper of Kansas, who drove a 1949 Lincoln to second place on the track, inherited the win.

Five months later, the eight-race inaugural season of the Strictly Stock division concluded with Bob Flock's victory on the half-mile dirt track at North Wilkesboro, North Carolina. The series crowned its first champion, Robert "Red" Byron of Atlanta, Georgia, who accumulated 842.5 points to 725 for second-place Lee Petty.

Bill France, the father of NASCAR.

PETTY STARTS A DYNASTY

Ironically, both Byron and Petty felt the wrath of Bill France during the 1950 season, when NASCAR stripped them of championship points for competing in non-sanctioned events. Petty lost the first 809 points he earned during the season and finished third in the final standings behind Bill Rexford and Glenn "Fireball" Roberts.

Though he failed to win a series championship before his death in 1964 from injuries sustained in a fiery crash at Charlotte Motor Speedway, the gregarious Roberts emerged as stock car racing's first real superstar. But it was Petty who founded a dynasty that would dominate NASCAR racing for the better part of three decades.

Petty won his first championship in 1954 in a Chrysler and followed that with back-to-back titles in 1958 (in an Oldsmobile) and 1959 (in a Plymouth). It was also in 1959 that Lee and Richard Petty became the first father-son combination to finish first and second in the same NASCAR race, when they took the checkered flag at Atlanta. A year later they repeated the feat in Pittsburgh, Pennsylvania.

Junior Johnson escapes through the rear window of his wrecked Pontiac at the Daytona Beach & Road Course in February 1956.

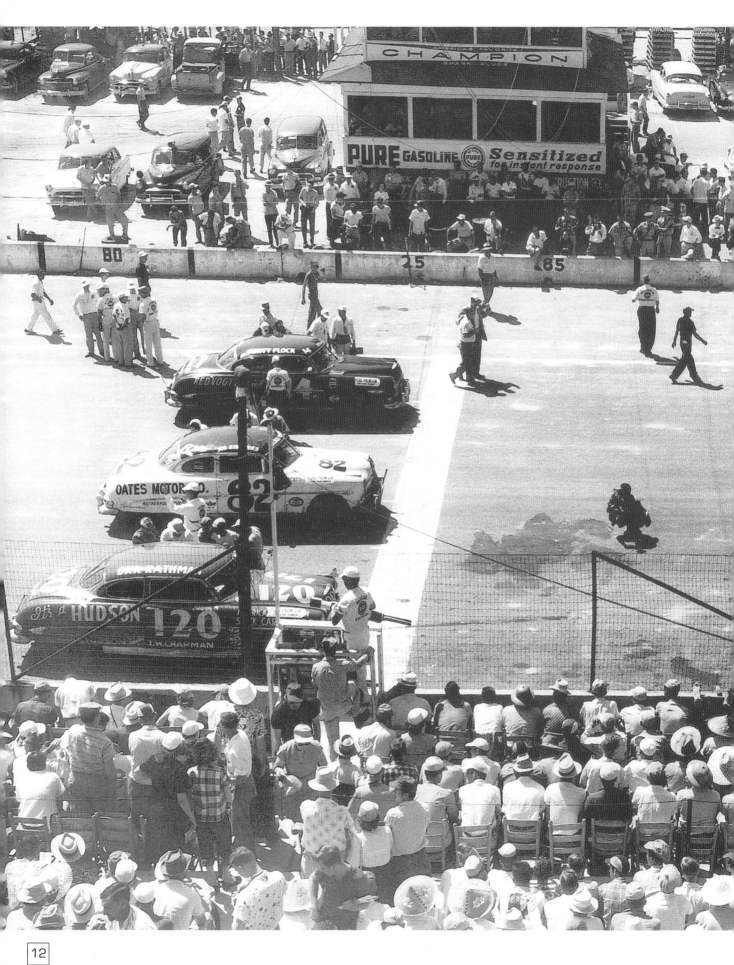

Richard Petty was a rookie during his father's championship season in 1958, but the man who would be "King" did not capture the first of his record 200 victories in NASCAR's elite series until 1960. Then the floodgates opened.

Petty won nine times and claimed the first of his seven series titles in 1964, but because of a Chrysler boycott resulting from France's decision to disallow the car maker's new hemi-head engine, Petty competed in just 14 races in 1965 and did not factor in the points race. Back in form in 1966, Petty won eight races and finished third in points behind David Pearson (who won 15 of the 42 events he entered) and James Hylton.

It was in 1967 that Petty left his indelible mark on the sport. With 27 victories and 38 top-fives in 48 races, the legend from Level Cross, North Carolina, won $150,000 and captured his second championship by more than 6,000 points over runner-up Hylton.

THE CROWNING OF THE KING

Even more remarkable was the mind-boggling winning streak Petty fashioned that year. On August 12 he finished three laps ahead of Jim Paschal in the Myers Brothers Memorial race at Bowman Gray Stadium in Winston-Salem, North Carolina. It wasn't until October 15 at Charlotte that Petty would lose another race.

His string of ten straight wins lasted two months and included the storied Southern 500 at Darlington Raceway in South Carolina. No other driver has come close to equalling that mark. To racing fans, Petty's winning streak is just as "untouchable" as Joe DiMaggio's 56-game hitting streak is to baseball aficionados.

Though Petty would win five more titles before retiring after the 1992 season, his exploits in 1967 brought stock car racing squarely into the national spotlight. If Arnold Palmer propelled golf to the forefront in the 1960s, then Petty multiplied the popularity of stock car racing exponentially during the same decade. It is no accident that both Palmer and Petty are known in their respective sports simply as "The King."

The 1960s also saw the expansion of NASCAR's appeal in the consciousness of the auto racing community as a whole. The lure of intense competition drew such luminaries as Mario Andretti, Al Unser and A.J. Foyt—renowned for their open-wheeled exploits at Indianapolis—to the super-speedways of the South. Andretti won the Daytona 500 in 1967, Foyt in 1972. To this day, Andretti remains the only driver ever to have won the Indianapolis 500, the Daytona 500 and the Formula One driving world championship.

The main story of the 1960s, though, was Petty, and it is a source of no small degree of irony that the King did not receive the live television exposure he deserved during his peak years as a driver. Though R.J. Reynolds signed on as Winston Cup's title sponsor in 1971 and brought the vast marketing capabilities of that company into the equation, NASCAR's main event, the Daytona 500, was not televised live until 1979—Petty's final championship season.

Nonetheless, that inaugural broadcast was a watershed event for the sport. With one lap remaining, Cale Yarborough, Winston Cup champion in 1976, 1977 and 1978, and the only driver ever to win three straight titles, battled Donnie Allison for the lead.

Yarborough attempted to pass Allison on the back-stretch, but Allison's blocking maneuver forced Yarborough

off the asphalt to the inside of the 2.5-mile superspeedwa. As Yarborough returned to the racing surface, the cars co lided, continued side-by-side, bumped several times an crashed in tandem into the third turn wall.

Mired in third place before the crash, Petty sped to serendipitous victory, narrowly beating Darrell Waltrip t the finish line. But the CBS cameras focused on the fistfigl that erupted between Yarborough and Bobby Allison, wh stopped on the backstretch to check on the condition of h: brother. Donnie soon joined the fray. That was mainstream America's introduction to big-time stock car racing.

EMERGENCE OF EARNHARDT

In effect, the 1979 championship was Petty's swan-song. H won a total of ten races in the following five years, but th last victory—his 200th—again claimed the attention of th sporting world. On July 4, 1984, with the president of th United States, Ronald Reagan, in attendance, Petty won th Firecracker 400 at Daytona and added to a career victor total that is unlikely ever to be eclipsed.

If 1979 provided Petty with his final championship, also served to introduce a brash young rookie fro Kannapolis, North Carolina to followers of the sport. With a aggressive driving style, that in turn impressed and annoye his fellow competitors, Dale Earnhardt won Winston Cup Rookie of the Year crown that season. A year later, he woul claim the first of his record-tying seven championships.

The 1980s brought the personalities of NASCAR in focus, from fast-talking Darrell Waltrip (nicknamed "Jaws for his loquaciousness), to "Million Dollar" Bill Elliott, fir winner of the Winston Million Bonus established by R. Reynolds. Add to the mix the irreverence of Tim Richmon (an enormously talented driver who contracted AIDS an died in 1989), the inexhaustible humor of Neil Bonnett (wh died in a practice crash at Daytona in 1994), the self-assu ance of Rusty Wallace, the dedication of Ricky Rudd, an the tenacity of Dave Marcis, a driver's driver who qualifie for his final Daytona 500 in 2002, at age 60.

But until Jeff Gordon claimed his first championship i 1995, Earnhardt was the dominant driver in Winston Cu for more than ten years. And though Earnhardt won h final series title in 1994, he continued to dominate the spo with his unrelenting will to win. Despite Gordon's prod

King Richard in all his glory.

The NEXTEL Cup: NASCAR's new trophy for 2004.

gious success, Earnhardt remained the primary focus of stock car racing until his death in the 2001 Daytona 500.

Earnhardt was a throwback to an earlier era. He was a master at getting the most from an ill-handling car. He was tight with a buck, thanks to a hard-scrabble upbringing that taught him the value of money. He inspired fanatic loyalty among his supporters and loathing among those who rooted against him. Because of Earnhardt's timely use of the "bump-and-run," the black No. 3 Chevy was the last thing another driver wanted to see in his rearview mirror.

And ironically, though Earnhardt steadfastly refused to wear a full-face crash helmet, his death has done more to promote safety enhancements in stock car racing than any other event in the history of the sport. With Earnhardt departed, it is Gordon, more than any other driver, who has carried NEXTEL Cup racing into the 21st century, and it is Gordon against whom pretenders to the throne will be measured.

The embodiment of the high-tech sophistication that now permeates the NEXTEL Cup Series, Gordon has enjoyed a meteoric ascendance. Assisted by crew chief and mechanical guru Ray Evernham during his first three championship seasons (1995, 1997 and 1998), Gordon silenced skeptics in 2001 by winning the title with second-

year crew chief Robbie Loomis (a veteran of Petty Enterprises) on the pit box.

Gordon is also at the vanguard of stock car racing's evolution toward multi-car teams. Gordon's car owner, Rick Hendrick, added a fourth team to his organization for 2002, to make room for rookie Jimmie Johnson, who quickly became a championship contender. Car owner Jack Roush has employed as many as five Winston Cup drivers at the same time. Evernham, who heads the flagship organization for Dodge, added talented rookie Kasey Kahne to his roster for the 2004 season, after Elliott announced his retirement as a full-time driver.

If the 2004 season brought new faces, it also brought fundamental change to the sport. NEXTEL replaced Winston as the title sponsor for NASCAR's foremost series, and the sanctioning body changed the format for determining the NEXTEL Cup champion. Instead of a season-long points competition, NASCAR inaugurated the "Chase for the NEXTEL Cup," with the top 10 drivers after 26 events (and any other drivers within 400 points of the leader) competing for the title over the final ten events.

It is against this backdrop that NASCAR's superstars of today vie for supremacy.

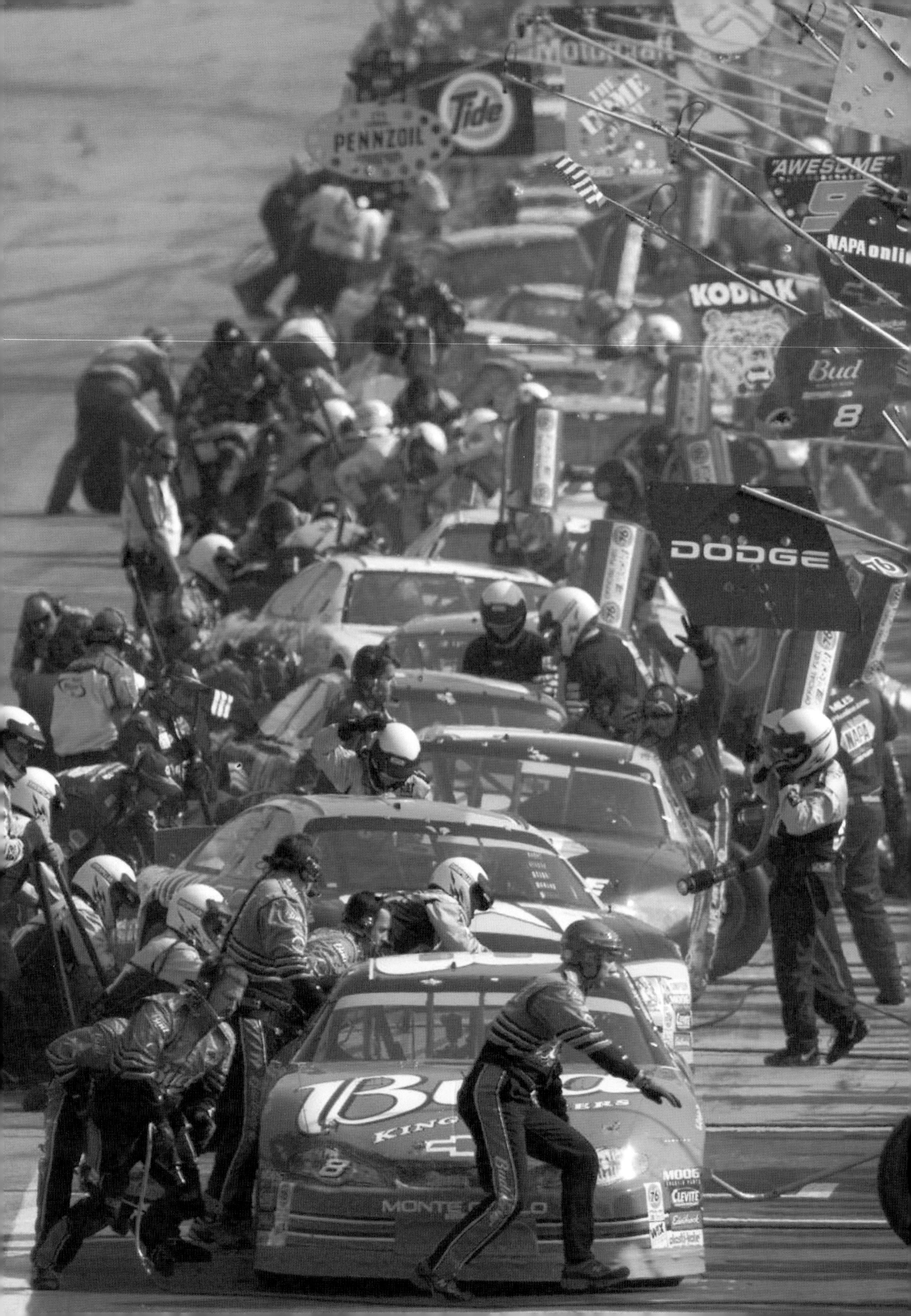

PENNZOIL
Tide
"AWESOME"
KODIAK
Bud
DODGE
MOOG
CLEVITE

The DRIVERS

What do NASCAR's superstars have in common? Without question, they all possess the ability to control a machine hurtling around a racetrack on the ragged edge between perfection and disaster. And to a man, they all enjoy the thrill of high-speed racing at close quarters, especially where an all-out dash to the checkered flag is concerned.

During the past decade, fans of NEXTEL Cup racing have gotten to know a new generation of NASCAR superstars. Foremost among them is Jeff Gordon, a racing prodigy who began competing before he reached first grade. At age 33, Gordon already has four championships to his credit, and in all likelihood, he will threaten the record seven titles shared by Richard Petty and Dale Earnhardt before his career is over.

Dale Earnhardt Jr. is continuing the tradition of his famous father, who died before his time in a last-lap crash at the 2001 Daytona 500. A driver in his father's image, Junior is an aggressive charger who has captivated the stock car racing audience with his fearless style.

If ever there was a driver who is "driven," it would have to be tempestuous Tony Stewart. In 1999 Stewart accomplished what no other NEXTEL Cup rookie had done before—he won three races. In 2002 he won the series championship for Joe Gibbs Racing.

There are other young guns to cheer for, even if they lack the pedigree of a Gordon, Earnhardt or Stewart. Kasey Kahne, Jamie McMurray and Casey Mears, for example, all possess formidable talent. The follow in the footsteps of such young stars as Kevin Harvick, who won the first Vinston Cup race he entered in 2001, at Atlanta, after taking over for the departed Dale Earnhardt.

Driving for owner Jack Roush, Matt Kenseth edged Earnhardt Jr. for the Rookie of the Year title in 2000 and went on to win the series championship in 2003. Kurt Busch, another Roush protégé, had a solid inaugural season in 2001 and quickly blossomed into a championship contender. Ryan Newman and Jimmie Johnson, a pair of rookies in 2002, both qualified for the "Chase for the NEXTEL Cup" in 2004. Johnson won the pole for the 2002 Daytona 500 in his first attempt to qualify for the race.

Let's not forget the experienced 30-somethings and 40-somethings who still can provide ample thrills for their supporters. Rusty Wallace (the master of the short tracks), Dale Jarrett (with the mighty engines of Robert Yates powering his cars), Bobby Labonte (one of stock car racing's most consistent drivers), and brother Terry Labonte (a mainstay at Hendrick Motorsports) all are former series champions. But Wallace and Terry Labonte announced their impending retirements in 2004, another indication of the changing of the guard.

Two-time Daytona 500 winner Sterling Martin saw his career rejuvenated in 2001 after Chip Ganassi bought majority interest in Felix Sabates' SABCO racing teams and switched to Dodge. Ricky Rudd, who won at least one race per year from 1983 through 1998, battled Gordon for the 2001 title before moving from Robert Yates Racing to the Wood Brothers in 2003. Michael Waltrip broke a 462-race winless drought with his victory in the 2001 Daytona 500.

Ward Burton, Joe Nemechek, Jeremy Mayfield and Elliott Sadler all have NEXTEL Cup victories to their credit. Finding a NASCAR superstar to cheer for isn't the problem. The difficulty lies in deciding which superstar to support.

The most frenetic 15 seconds in major league sports—a pit stop under a caution flag.

Greg **BIFFLE**

If the old saying is true, namely that slow and steady wins the race, then Greg Biffle may be moving closer to a NEXTEL Cup championship.

The Vancouver, Washington, driver is unique in NASCAR racing. He's the only competitior ever to win championships in both the Craftsman Truck Series and the Busch Series. He accomplished that feat after becoming the only driver ever to win Rookie of the Year titles in both series.

Now there's only one more world for Biffle to conquer: NEXTEL Cup.

Biffle is hardly an overnight sensation. From 1994 through 1997, he paid his dues in NASCAR's Weekly Racing Series for late model stock cars, winning track titles in West Richland, Washington and Portland, Oregon. Biffle was so dominant in late models that in 1995 he won 27 of the 43 races he started.

Then began the slow, steady progression to NEXTEL Cup racing under the tutelage of owner Jack Roush. In 1998 Biffle was Rookie of the Year in the Craftsman Truck Series. A year later he won nine races and finished second in points. In 2000 Biffle claimed the Truck Series title, giving Roush his first NASCAR championship.

Biffle graduated to the Busch Series in 2001 and earned Rookie of the Year honors in a Roush Racing Ford. At the same time, he continued to enhance his reputation as a fearless, aggressive driver and picked up five victories in the series. The following season brought a Busch Series championship.

Biffle also got his first taste of NEXTEL Cup racing in 2002, but only one of his seven starts came in a car owned by Roush. Biffle replaced Bobby Hamilton in Andy Petree's No. 55 Cheverolet for four races, and he also did spot duty

STATS (SINCE 2000)

YEAR	STARTS	WINS	TOP 5	TOP 10	MONEY
2000	did not compete				
2001	did not compete				
2002	7	0	0	0	$ 394,773
2003	35	1	3	6	$2,805,673
2004	36	2	4	8	$3,523,342
CAREER	**78**	**3**	**7**	**14**	**$6,723,788**

for two races in the No. 44 Petty Enterprises Dodge.

It took Biffle half a season of full-time NEXTEL Cup racing to capture his first event. In his 23rd career start in the series, Biffle made the most of a fuel-mileage gamble in winning the Pepsi 400 at Daytona International Speedway in July of 2003. In another unique twist, Biffle was the only first-time winner in NEXTEL Cup that year.

For the first time in any of NASCAR's top three touring divisions, however, Biffle failed to claim the Rookie of the Year title. He lost a closely contested battle to precocious "young gun" Jamie McMurray.

When the series visited Daytona for the season-opening Daytona 500 in February of 2004, Biffle underscored his prowess on restrictor-place tracks by qualifying on the pole. And though he suffered through an inconsisten season, he won the August race at Michigan from the 24th starting position.

In 2004, Biffle ran a full Busch Series schedule in addition to his full-time NEXTEL Cup commitments. To Biffle's way of thinking, the travel involved in competing for two championships may have diluted his focus on NEXTEL Cup. As the 2004 season neared its end, Biffle was contemplating a limited Busch Series schedule for 2005.

If his focus is uncompromised, Biffle could become the only driver to have won championships in the Craftsman Truck Series, Busch Series AND NEXTEL Cup.

16

Birthdate: December 23, 1969
Birthplace: Vancouver, WA
Team: Roush Racing
Sponsor: National Guard/Subway
Owner: Jack Roush
Crew Chief: Doug Richert
Car Make: Ford

Greg Biffle is already a successful racing driver

19

Dave **BLANEY**

If nothing else, Dave Blaney has learned to adapt to change.

Like former Sprint Car champion Steve Kinser before him, Blaney has struggled to find a consistent level of performance in the stock car ranks. On the other hand, he has displayed, on more than a few occasions, the depth of his driving talent.

Blaney won the 1995 World of Outlaws championship and was named Sprint Car Driver of the Year that same season. In 1999, he finished seventh in the Busch Series standings despite missing one event due to a scheduling conflict with one of his five starts in the Winston Cup. He won four Busch Series poles, posted 13 top-10s and twice finished second in 1999, at Atlanta in March and at Darlington in September. In his five Winston Cup events with Bill Davis Racing, he qualified fourth and finished 23rd at Homestead for his best results in each category.

Blaney's rookie season in the Winston Cup (2000) was an up-and-down affair. Though he claimed a pair of top-10 finishes, he failed to complete seven races. Davis switched his teams from Pontiac to Dodge for 2001, and despite the complications inherent in a change-over from one make to another, Blaney can point to one formidable accomplishment during his sophomore season—he qualified for all 36 Winston Cup events. Three times he finished sixth—at Texas in April, in the Pepsi 400 at Daytona in July and at Rockingham in October—for his best results of the campaign. The 2001 season also brought a career-best finish in the points standings—22nd, one notch ahead of two-time series champion Terry Labonte—and a career-best year for prize money, more than $1.8 million.

But 2002 brought more change for Blaney. He left Davis and signed on with the Jasper Engines, replacing Robert Pressley in the No. 77 car. That move also meant a switch to

Ford and the chance to work with crew chief Ryan Pemberton. "I'm going to try them all out before I find one I like," was Blaney's tongue-in-cheek comment about the frequent changes in manufacturers.

Blaney finished a respectable 19th in points in 2002, posting five top-10s against three DNFs, but instability in his job situation continued. By the time the 2003 season began, Pemberton had given way to Robert "Bootie" Barker in the crew chief's role; by 2004, Blaney was out of a full-time ride—and looking for more than the fill-in roles he occupied in the first year of the Chase for the NEXTEL Cup.

Blaney competed in his first NEXTEL Cup race in a Pontiac, but not in one owned by Bill Davis. Before 1999, his only Cup experience had come at Rockingham in 1992, where he completed 371 of 492 laps in the Steve Hovel Pontiac and finished 31st. That was the beginning, but what Blaney hopes for now more than anything is a happy ending.

Blaney hasn't abandoned Sprint Cars: he owns the World of Outlaws team for which his brother, Dale Blaney, drives.

STATS (SINCE 2000)

YEAR	STARTS	WINS	TOP 5	TOP 10	MONEY
2000	33	0	0	2	$1,272,689
2001	36	0	0	6	$1,827,296
2002	36	0	0	5	$2,677,710
2003	36	0	1	4	$2,828,690
2004	16	0	0	0	$1,461,640
CAREER	**157**	**0**	**1**	**17**	**$10,068,025**

Easy-going and pensive off the track, Dave Blaney is a charger behind the wheel

Birthdate: October 29, 1962

Birthplace: Sharon, PA

Team: Jasper Motorsports

Sponsor: Jasper Engines & Transmissions

Owners: Doug Bawel, Mark Harrah, Mark Wallace

Crew Chief: Ryan Pemberton

Car: Ford

Jeff **BURTON**

For Jeff Burton, the 2001 season was a harbinger of change, but that change would not occur until 2004. Most drivers would have taken Burton's 2001 season and walked away satisfied. After all, the Virginia driver won two races—the prestigious Coca-Cola 600 at Charlotte and Checker Auto Parts/Dura-Lube 500 at Phoenix. In the process the younger of the two Burton brothers over $3.7 million.

But for Burton, 2001 was a step backwards, a change of direction in a career that had been an unrelenting ascent to the top level of his sport. Burton was 10th in the NEXTEL Cup standings, but that was the first time since 1996 that he had finished outside the top five. The 2001 season also broke a streak of successes in which each year had been better than its predecessor.

Driving for the Stavola Brothers team, Burton won the Winston Cup Rookie of the Year crown in 1994. After spending the 1995 season with the Stavolas, Burton jumped at the chance to drive for Jack Roush in 1996. He has been with Roush ever since.

Burton won his first Winston Cup race at Texas in April of 1997, and before the season was over, he had collected his second and third victories—at New Hampshire and Martinsville. He was the model of consistency with 13 top-five finishes and 18 top-10s. His first foray into the elite top 10 in the points standings was also his first visit to the rarefied air of the top five; Burton was fourth at the end of the year.

The 1998 season brought two more wins, 18 top-fives, 23 top-10s and a fifth-place points finish, but that was just an indication of what was to come in 1999. With six victories—at Charlotte, New Hampshire, Las Vegas,

STATS (SINCE 2000)

YEAR	STARTS	WINS	TOP 5	TOP 10	MONEY
2000	34	4	15	22	$5,959,439
2001	36	2	8	16	$4,230,727
2002	36	0	5	14	$4,244,856
2003	36	0	3	11	$4,384,752
2004	36	0	2	6	$3,695,075
CAREER	**367**	**17**	**91**	**150**	**$35,283,182**

Rockingham, and both Darlington races (including th coveted Southern 500), Burton earned a career-bes $5,725,399 and another fifth in the season standings.

With 2000 came Burton's highest finish in th points—third—and four more victories. In one of thos wins, New Hampshire, he accomplished the rare fea of leading all 300 laps.

Not surprisingly, Burton was considered a formida ble contender for the Winston Cup championship i 2001. Surprisingly, he wasn't a threat. Never a stron qualifier, Burton had always been able to count on hi ability to work his way to the front during the course a race. In 2001, his Fords lacked their customary muscle

"Even though we did put a string of good race together toward the end of the year... we didn't lea enough laps, which means we weren't as fast as w needed to be," Burton said of the disappointing seasor

Burton's fortunes, however, worsened in 2002, whe he failed to finish five races and slipped to 12th i points. A crew chief change from Frank Stoddard t Paul Andrews didn't help matters. By the start of th 2004 season, Burton was driving the No. 99 For

30

Birthdate: June 29, 1967
Birthplace: South Boston, VA
Team: Richard Childress Racing
Sponsor: Cingular
Owner: Richard Childress
Crew Chief: Kevin Hamlin
Car Make: Chevrolet

without benefit of a primary sponsor, and his days with the Roush organization appeared numbered.

Released by Roush during the season, Burton signed on with Richard Childress Racing as the driver of the No. 30 AOL Chevrolet and seemed rejuvenated by the prospect of driving for the former owner of

Jeff Burton hopes to get back to winning ways behind the wheel of the #30 AOL Chevrolet.

Dale Earnhardt's legendary No. 3 Chevy. In the August race at Bristol, Burton posted his best finish of the 2004 season—fourth.

Ward BURTON

Everybody in the NASCAR garage does an impression of Ward Burton, because his unmistakable slow Virginia drawl is so much fun to mimic.

Burton's laid-back personality matches his speech pattern, until he climbs behind the wheel. That is where his competitive fire manifests itself, the same sort of drive that earned him top ranking on Hargrave Military Academy's rifle team during his high school days in Virginia.

On the track, Burton is a charger, as he has demonstrated consistently during his Winston Cup career. In his first season, racing for A.G. Dillard in 1994, Burton won the pole for the October race in Charlotte. After moving to Bill Davis Racing for the final nine races of the 1995 season, Burton posted his first Winston Cup victory in the fall race at Rockingham.

His next victory would not come until the March 2000 race at Darlington, though Burton did accumulate three second-place finishes in 1999. In fact, Burton found himself in the championship mix early in 2000 with eight top-10s in the first 13 races. At that time he was second in the Winston Cup points standings, but the balance of the season wasn't as kind to the No. 22 Caterpillar team. By season's end Burton had fallen to tenth in the standings. And 2000 also marked the first time in five years that Burton failed to win a pole.

With Davis Racing's switch from Pontiac to Dodge in 2001 came the most significant victory of Burton's career— a win at the Southern 500 in Darlington. That race, however, was the high watermark in an otherwise inconsistent year that saw Burton fall to 14th in Winston Cup points.

But the driver who jokingly refers to himself as "Ranger Rick" because of his very serious involvement in wildlife preservation and conservation added the most important milestone to his resume in 2002. Burton won the season-opening Daytona 500, but that was the highlight of an erratic year. Though he also won at New Hampshire and collected a career-best $4,899,884 in earnings, Burton failed to finish nine races and fell to 25th in the final points standings.

A lackluster effort in 2003 convinced Burton and Davis to go separate ways, and Burton signed on with Gene Haas as driver of the NetZero Chevrolet. The first 30 races of the 2004 season, however, brought only one top 10.

But Burton is a talented driver with five NEXTEL Cup victories to his credit, and it's too soon to write him off. With sufficient financing and the right equipment, Burton could still make a run for the NEXTEL Cup.

STATS (SINCE 2000)

YEAR	STARTS	WINS	TOP 5	TOP 10	MONEY
2000	34	1	4	17	$2,699,604
2001	36	1	6	10	$3,633,692
2002	36	2	3	8	$4,899,884
2003	36	0	0	4	$3,628,600
2004	34	0	0	3	$2,471,941
CAREER	356	5	24	82	$24,023,735

Birthdate: October 25, 1961
Birthplace: South Boston, VA
Team: Haas CNC Racing*
Sponsor: NetZero*
Owner: Gene Haas*
Crew Chief: Bill Ingle*
Car: Chevrolet*

Ward Burton's NASCAR career has had many highs and lows, but with a little luck he may get back on track.

*until November 2004

Kurt BUSCH

The unqualified success of such young drivers as Jeff Gordon and Tony Stewart increases the pressure on other owners to sign the next "young gun" to a NEXTEL Cup contract. That temptation can sometimes lead to the premature promotion of an inexperienced driver to NASCAR's highest level.

When Jack Roush announced in 2000 that he was adding Kurt Busch to his roster of NEXTEL Cup drivers, there were skeptics. After all, Busch had come to the owner's attention during a series of tryouts known as the "Gong Shows." Prior to signing on with Roush as a trainee in NASCAR's Craftsman Truck Series, Busch had limited, albeit successful racing experience—in Legends Cars, Dwarf Cars and NASCAR's Featherlite Southwest Tour, where he won he series championship in 1999.

Busch soon made believers of his doubters, and his deep reservoir of driving talent proved more than enough to offset his sketchy resume. He won four Truck Series races in 2000 to go with a pair of top-10 qualifying efforts in the seven NEXTEL Cup races events he entered as preparation for a full schedule in 2001. And by the end of 2004, he was NEXTEL Cup champion. So much for the skeptics.

Sure, there were growing pains in his first full season of Cup racing, but Busch showed flashes of brilliance. He posted his first top-five finish in the seventh race of the season, at Texas, where he crossed the finish line in fourth place. Two races later, he finished third at the world's fastest closed course, the 2.66-mile tri-oval at Talladega. A fifth-place at the Brickyard 400 in August proved Busch could also negotiate a flat track.

Predictably inconsistent during his freshman season,

STATS (SINCE 2000)

YEAR	STARTS	WINS	TOP 5	TOP 10	MONEY
2000	7	0	0	0	$311,915
2001	35	0	3	6	$2,170,629
2002	36	4	12	20	$5,105,394
2003	36	4	9	14	$5,587,384
2004	36	3	10	21	$4,120,332
CAREER	**150**	**11**	**34**	**61**	**$17,303,683**

Busch was 27th in the points, but he finished ahead of a number of series regulars, among them Todd Bodine, Joe Nemechek and John Andretti.

Busch entered the 2002 season with an optimistic outlook, buoyed his taste of success in 2001. Perhaps his approach to the qualifying races at Daytona also sums up his attitude as a driver.

"I love the pressure," Busch says. "It's what I live off of. I love to be the guy that the pressure is on, to have it on my shoulders so I can pull through and do it for the team."

Busch handled the pressure of the first Chase for the NEXTEL Cup like a veteran. Despite a broken wheel in the final race of the 2004 season, he rallied for a fifth-place finish and edged Jimmie Johnson for the title by eight points.

Busch isn't exactly mainstream when it comes the NASCAR community. He prefers alternative rock music (Metallica in particular) to country and western, the stock car racing staple. He's also an avid Chicago Cubs fan.

Fortunately, Busch didn't find the championship as elusive as the Cubs have.

97

Birthdate: August 4, 1978
Birthplace: Las Vegas, NV
Team: Roush Racing
Sponsor: Sharpie/IRWIN Industrial Tools
Owner: Jack Roush
Crew Chief: Jimmy Fennig
Car Make: Ford

Kurt Busch let his driving do the talking for him in 2004—and it earned him the NEXTEL Cup.

Dale **EARNHARDT** JR

If there is one indelible snapshot of Dale Earnhardt Jr.'s young life, it is the celebration at Daytona in July of 2001—the third-generation driver standing atop his No. 8 Chevrolet, hugged by teammate Michael Waltrip.

Earnhardt had just sped to a dominating victory in the Pepsi 400, in effect conquering the speedway that had taken the life of his legendary father just five months earlier. For Junior, the victory was more than redemption. It was an indication to the world that he had learned to live with the pain of his loss and had translated that pain into performance.

It was Earnhardt's third NEXTEL Cup victory, and to that point, the defining moment in his short career.

"I had hard core emotions about going back after my father's death," Earnhardt says.

"Everybody knows the story. Had fun there and went to the race with a strong will; won the race and all of that, and with all that happened, I have said my piece with that place or straightened out any wrinkles we might have had in our relationship, so I look forward to going back—because I love Daytona. I always have, always will; going into that place, I probably won't have the same emotion as most people. Most people might be depressed or upset, but I'm going to keep on being upbeat and having a damn good time."

The Pepsi 400 was also a breakout victory for Earnhardt, who won twice more before the end of the season, at Dover and at Talladega. He finished eighth in the points standings.

Earnhardt embarked on his professional driving career at age 17. What other career path was the son of a seven-time NEXTEL Cup champion going to follow? In the early days, he raced against his brother Kerry and sister Kelley in late model stock cars.

His rise through the ranks of NASCAR's touring series was meteoric. In 1997, he entered eight Busch Series events. In 1998 he won the championship in that division. Earnhardt won six races and added another Busch Series title to his portfolio in 1999. By 2000, he was ready for a full-time ride in the NEXTEL Cup Series, in a car owned by his father.

Earnhardt's rookie season brought two victories, the first coming at Texas, the second at Richmond. More important, he proved he could perform at peak levels despite the onerous expectations that came with being his father's son. Ironically, Earnhardt did not win NEXTEL Cup's rookie-of-the-year crown, a feat accomplished by his father in 1979. Instead, the title went to Matt Kenseth, one of Roush Racing's young stars and a protégé of veteran Mark Martin.

Then came Daytona 2001, where Earnhardt chased Waltrip to the finish line while his father sat lifeless in his crumpled black No. 3 Chevy a few hundred yards behind. But as he says, Earnhardt Jr. has made his peace with Daytona. Now he looks ahead toward the championship he needs to establish his own legend.

"There's more to me, I think, professionally than just magazine covers and kick-ass sponsors and fun times," Earnhardt says, referring to his appearances in *Rolling Stone* and *People*, the latter of which included him on a list of "Sexiest Men." "I want to win championships and I like winning races. We celebrate ours and enjoy that. We look forward to winning more, but there's a side from just winning the championship and all the celebration and the extras and whatnot that come along with that.

"There's something to be said about having that

Birthdate: October 10, 1979
Birthplace: Kannapolis, NC
Team: Dale Earnhardt Incorporated
Sponsor: Budweiser
Owner: Teresa Earnhardt
Crew Chief: Tony Eury Jr.
Car Make: Chevrolet

Third-generation driver Dale Earnhardt Jr. seems well-equipped to carry the torch passed on by his legendary father.

asterisk beside your name for the rest of your life and the rest of the time in the books that says you were champion sometime in your life. So that's something I'd like to be a part of. I can see that I have a great opportunity to really take it to several levels and to be somebody that maybe is in the same sentence with several of the greats in the sport down the road — so I need to win some championships."

Earnhardt came close in 2004. He qualified for the first Chase for the NEXTEL Cup and remained in contention until the 10th and final race of the Chase. But a 23rd-place

I want to win championships and I like winning races.

finish at Homestead-Miami Speedway cost him any chance he may have had for the title. Earnhardt finished fifth in the final standings, 138 points behind champion Kurt Busch.

The No. 8 Budweiser Chevrolet has become a dominant force at NASCAR's two restrictor-plate racetracks, Daytona and Talladega.

STATS (SINCE 2000)

YEAR	STARTS	WINS	TOP 5	TOP 10	MONEY
2000	34	2	3	5	$2,801,881
2001	36	3	9	15	$5,827,542
2002	36	2	11	16	$4,970,034
2003	36	2	13	21	$6,880,807
2004	36	6	16	21	$7,121,380
CAREER	183	15	52	79	$27,763,739

Brendan GAUGHAN

Don't bet against Brendan Gaughan. You'll be playing against the house.

Gaughan, of course, is the son of Michael Gaughan, a major player in the casino business in Las Vegas. The truck Gaughan drove in NASCAR's Craftsman Truck Series in 2002 and 2003 bore the insignia of the Orleans Hotel, one of the Gaughan family's properties.

Brendan himself is well versed in the casino business, having worked a variety of jobs at the hotel, from busboy to dealer. But the job at which Gaughan excels is that of driver, though his initial transition to the NEXTEL Cup Series was not without its share of growing pains.

Appropriately, given his hometown, Gaughan began racing in the desert. Before he made a career move to the asphalt ovals of stock car racing, Gaughan won three world titles in the off-road ranks. His affinity for racing, however, didn't prevent him from graduating from Georgetown University in Washington, D.C., with a degree in business management.

While at Georgetown, Gaughan played basketball for renowned coach John Thompson and was part of two Big East regular-season championship teams. In each of his four seasons, the Hoyas qualified for the NCAA tournament. The multitalented Gaughan was also an all-conference selection in football.

After back-to-back stock car championships in the Winston West Series in 2000 and 2001, Gaughan turned to NASCAR's touring Craftsman Truck Series in 2002. He won both races at Texas Motor Speedway that year, but Gaughan saved his breakout performance for 2003.

In the tightest four-way championship race in Truck Series history, Gaughan appeared the likely winner of the title until a late-race crash in the season's final event at Homestead-Miami Speedway relegated him to fourth in points, 49 behind series champion Travis Kvapil.

But there was no doubt that Gaughan had the dominant truck in 2003. He won a series-best six races and held the points lead for eight straight weeks before the final event. His spectacular season included three consecutive poles and 14 top-five finishes in 25 races.

Gaughan also sparked controversy during his Truck Series career by betting on himself at long odds at a rival casino. Gaughan won the race and collected the bet but also earned an admonition from NASCAR.

His performance behind the wheel earned him a full-time ride in the No. 77 Jasper/Penske Dodge for 2004, but the jump to NEXTEL Cup was far from seamless. Not until the 10th race of the season did Gaughan post his first top 10, a sixth at California Speedway. His first top five came 19 events later, when he finished fourth at Talladega. Gaughan's qualifying efforts, however, showed promise. In the first 15 races, he started in the top eight six times.

It's true that Gaughan hasn't found short-term success in NEXTEL Cup. But don't bet against his long-term results. In the long run, after all, the odds are always in favor of the house.

STATS (SINCE 2000)

YEAR	STARTS	WINS	TOP 5	TOP 10	MONEY
2000	did not compete				
2001	did not compete				
2002	did not compete				
2003	did not compete				
2004	36	0	1	4	$2,929,396
CAREER	**36**	**0**	**1**	**4**	**$2,929,396**

77

Birthdate: July 10, 1975

Birthplace: Las Vegas, NV

Team: Penske/Jasper Racing

Sponsor: Kodak/Jasper Engines

Owner: Douglas Bawel

Crew Chief: Shane Wilson

Car: Dodge

Brendan Gaughan: On his way to NEXTEL Cup success

Jeff GORDON

It's difficult to believe that a driver who won three NEXTEL Cup championships and claimed more than 50 victories before his 29th birthday still would have much to prove—but that was the case with Jeff Gordon.

Despite the phenomenal success he had enjoyed before the 2000 season, NASCAR's *Wunderkind* had his doubters. There were those who believed that most of the credit for Gordon's formidable results belonged to the Hendrick Motorsports organization (with its seemingly limitless resources) and the know-how of crew chief Ray Evernham, who made the calls from the pits in each of Gordon's championship runs, in 1995, 1997 and 1998.

The nay-sayers were convinced that Evernham's departure at the end of the 1999 season to spearhead the return of Dodge to NEXTEL Cup racing would diminish the magnitude of Gordon's stardom. In 2000, it appeared the doubters might be right. Gordon struggled as he and new crew chief Robbie Loomis began the acclimation process. Gordon also had a new "over-the-wall gang" to deal with in the pits, after the defection of the nucleus of the vaunted "Rainbow Warriors" to Robert Yates Racing.

Nevertheless, Gordon managed three victories in his first season with Loomis, a long-time crew chief at Petty Enterprises. Though he won at Talladega, Sears Point and Richmond, Gordon had not finished a season with fewer than seven victories since 1994, his second year with Hendrick Motorsports. His ninth-place finish in points was his worst since a 14th in 1993.

In 2001, however, Gordon silenced the skeptics who had failed to take sufficient notice of his own prodigious talent

STATS (SINCE 2000)					
YEAR	STARTS	WINS	TOP 5	TOP 10	MONEY
2000	34	3	11	22	$3,001,144
2001	36	6	18	24	$10,879,757
2002	36	3	13	20	$6,154,475
2003	36	3	15	20	$6,622,002
2004	36	5	16	25	$6,437,665
CAREER	**401**	**69**	**190**	**254**	**$64,962,722**

behind the wheel. The season brought not only a fourth NEXTEL Cup title for Gordon but also a variety of other significant milestones. Gordon claimed six victories, including an unprecedented third win in the Brickyard 400. He won for the first time at Las Vegas and captured the inaugural event at Kansas City, bringing to 20 the number of different racetracks on which he had scored at least one victory. Gordon won $10,879,757 in prize money, breaking the record of $9,306,584 he set in 1998. He passed the late Dale Earnhardt for the lead in career earnings and now heads the all-time list with $64,962,722. In 2001, he led 2,320 laps—more than twice the total of any other driver. At age 30, Gordon became the youngest driver to win four series championships.

Suddenly, Gordon's detractors were touting his chances to equal or break the record seven NEXTEL Cup titles shared by Richard Petty and Earnhardt. For Gordon, though, winning was nothing new. It was expected. The Vallejo, Ca., native had been driving racecars since kindergarten. In 1979, at age 8, he won his first national championship in quarter midgets. After winning the 1990 USAC Midget title, he moved from open-wheeled cars to NASCAR's Busch Series. Gordon was Rookie of the Year on stock car racing's junior circuit in 1991, but he still had time to capture the USAC

24

Birthdate: August 9, 1971
Birthplace: Vallejo, CA
Team: Hendrick Motorsports
Sponsor: DuPont
Owner: Rick Hendrick
Crew Chief: Robbie Loomis
Car: Chevrolet

In a snowstorm of confetti, Jeff Gordon exults in his fourth Winston Cup championship.

Jeff **GORDON**

Silver Crown championship that same season.

In 1992, he won three races and a series-record 11 poles driving a Busch car. That was all the seasoning he needed to begin his meteoric rise to the top of the NEXTEL Cup standings. His first full season in NEXTEL Cup was auspicious; though he failed to win a race in 1993, Gordon captured his first NEXTEL Cup pole at Charlotte and posted seven top-five finishes.

The following season brought a pair of victories in two of stock car racing's most prestigious events—the Coca-Cola 600 at Charlotte and the inaugural Brickyard 400 at Indianapolis. After those two wins came the deluge, which culminated in the championship run of 1998, when Gordon tied Petty's modern-era record of 13 victories in a single season. (The "modern era" dates to 1972, the first year of

I think I've become a smarter race car driver.

Winston's sponsorship of NASCAR's foremost series).

With 69 career victories through the 2004 season, Gordon is the leader among active drivers in that category. To put that accomplishment in perspective, consider that he is comfortably ahead of drivers who have been competing in NEXTEL Cup since the mid-1970s—Bill Elliott, Ricky Rudd and his own teammate, Terry Labonte, for example. Rusty Wallace, who made his NEXTEL Cup debut in 1980, is second on the active list with 55.

Though Gordon won five times in 2004, he fell just short in his drive for a fifth championship. In a title race that wasn't decided until the final lap of the final race, Gordon finished third in points, just 16 behind winner Kurt Busch.

Gordon believes his uncanny ability to communicate the handling characteristics of his No. 24 Chevrolet is crucial to the team's success. "I don't think that my skills as a driver, my actual talent has gotten better," Gordon said. "I think I just have gotten better at communicating... I think I've become a smarter racecar driver."

Jeff Gordon is as comfortable in a night race at Bristol as on the banks of a superspeedway or the tight corners of a road course.

Robby GORDON

One of the most versatile drivers on the NEXTEL Cup circuit—and one of the most mercurial—Robby Gordon has yet to find a consistent level of excellence in NASCAR's premier division.

ake no mistake. There have been flashes of brilliance. In 2001, Gordon claimed his first NEXTEL Cup victory in the September race at New Hampshire, after signing on with Richard Childress Racing during the second half of the season.

In 2002, in his first full season of NEXTEL Cup racing, Gordon failed to win a race, but he notched five top 10s and finished a respectable 20th in the final points standings. The 2002 season was also noteworthy for a wholesale pit crew swap in June between Gordon and teammate Kevin Harvick, both of whom were struggling at the time. The switch brought Harvick's crew chief, Kevin Hamlin, to the Gordon team and sent Gordon's crew chief, Gil Martin, to Harvick's.

After the crew chief change, Gordon rallied during the second half of the season, and the improvement continued in 2003. A road course specialist, thanks to his background in open-wheeled racecars and off-road vehicles, Gordon won the road course races at Sonoma and Watkins Glen to bring his career NEXTEL Cup victory total to three. He also improved his points finish to 16th.

During the 2004 season, however, progress stalled. Despite an occasional strong run, the performance of the No. 31 was uneven, to say the least, and Gordon announced that he would leave Childress and form his own team for 2005.

That's not a novel approach for Gordon, who likes to run his own show. In 2000, Gordon fielded his own cars for 17 NEXTEL Cup races with limited success. Nine years

earlier, Gordon had made his NEXTEL Cup debut, competing in two races for car owner Junie Donlavey. Gordon raced once in 1993 for Robert Yates, after the death of Davey Allison in a helicopter crash, and competed in one event for Kranefuss-Haas the following year.

In 1995 the California driver focused his attention on open-wheeled races, winning IndyCar races at Detroit and Phoenix and finishing fifth in CART Series points. In 1996 he posted four victories in the SCORE Off-Road Trophy Truck Series and won the championship. In both 1996 and 1997, he finished second in the IROC Series.

Throughout the 1990s, Gordon raced in the Indianapolis 500, and in 1999 he came within an eyelash of winning of winning the storied race. Gordon led 33 laps near the end of the race, only to run out of fuel on the final circuit. He finished fourth. On May 26, 2002, he drove in both the Indianapolis 500 and Coca-Cola 600 NEXTEL Cup race in Charlotte, commuting between the two tracks by airplane. Gordon fished eighth at Indy and 16th at Lowe's Motor Speedway.

His success in other forms of racing, however, hasn't translated to prominence in NEXTEL Cup. Perhaps his excitable temperament has held him back. After all, there's no denying Gordon's talent as a driver.

Perhaps his "privateer" effort in 2005 will elevate Gordon's stock car racing career.

STATS (SINCE 2000)

YEAR	STARTS	WINS	TOP 5	TOP 10	MONEY
2000	17	0	1	2	$620,781
2001	17	1	2	3	$1,371,900
2002	36	0	1	5	$3,342,703
2003	36	2	4	10	$4,157,064
2004	36	0	2	6	$3,945,545
CAREER	170	3	11	27	$14,172,007

31

Birthdate: January 2, 1969

Birthplace: Bleeflower, CA

Team: Team Gordon

Sponsor: TBA

Owner: Robby Gordon

Crew Chief: TBA

Car: TBA

Robby Gordon's 2004 drive, Cingular Wireless Chelvrolet.

Bobby HAMILTON Jr

There's no heredity-versus-environment argument where Bobby Hamilton Jr. is concerned. The Nashville, Tenn., driver has the benefit of both influences.

The son of NASCAR veteran Bobby Hamilton, the younger Hamilton inherited the genes that have kept his father active in various forms of racing for 15 years. And as the elder Hamilton has found a comfortable home in NASCAR's Craftsman Truck Series (where he is a perennial contender for the championship), Bobby Jr. has ascended to the NEXTEL Cup Series as the full-time driver of Cal Wells' No. 32 Tide Chevrolet.

He also grew up in a racing environment. Hamilton Sr. launched his son's racing career in 1993 with the gift of a 1971 Ford Pinto. A year later, and with the Pinto benefiting from considerable work in the Hamilton's garage, 16-year-old Bobby Jr. won the track championship in the mini-modified division at Highland Rim Speedway near Ridgetop, Tenn.

In 1998 he began driving more powerful machines. Competing in the ARCA Supercar Series, Hamilton posted five top-five finishes in his first six starts. That same year he competed in the Busch Series for the first time, with his debut coming at North Carolina Speedway in Rockingham, N.C., on October 31.

By 2000 Hamilton was a Busch Series regular. In the spring race at Talladega, he earned his first top-five finish (fourth). At Homestead, he won his first Busch Series pole. Driving a car owned by his father, Hamilton also made his first NEXTEL Cup start in 2000. He finished 30th at Homestead in his inaugural event and followed that with a 28th-place result in the season finale in Atlanta.

The next three years saw steady improvement in the Busch Series. Hamilton was 17th in points in 2001 and eighth in 2002. In 2003 he made a phenomenal late-season run to finish fourth in the standings. Winner of a series-best four races for Team Rensi Motorsports' No. 25 U.S. Marine Corps Ford, Hamilton took the checkered flag in two of the season's final five races and finished third in the other three. Hamilton's meteoric rise through the points standings coincided with the addition of crew chief Harold Holly to the team.

But the magic didn't continue into 2004. Hamilton failed to win in 23 starts and was released by Rensi, although he stood eighth in points at the time. It didn't take Hamilton long to find a home in the NEXTEL Cup Series, though. He jumped into the vacant seat of the Tide ride and soon gave fans of NASCAR's elite series a few glimpses of his talent.

At Richmond, Hamilton started 22nd and improved to 11th place by the time the race ended. At Lowe's Motor Speedway, one of NASCAR's most difficult tracks, he qualified 11th and finished 15th.

Holly continues to work with Hamilton in his new situation. Veteran crew chief Mike Beam is also part of the equation at Wells' PPI Motorsports. With that kind of experience and experience behind him, Hamilton should flourish. There's no doubt he has the right bloodlines.

STATS (SINCE 2000)

YEAR	STARTS	WINS	TOP 5	TOP 10	MONEY
2000	2	0	0	0	$82,390
2001	10	0	0	0	$546,847
2002	did not compete				
2003	2	0	0	0	$128,725
2004	17	0	0	0	$1,259,210
CAREER	**31**	**0**	**0**	**0**	**$2,017,172**

32

Birthdate: January 8, 1978

Birthplace: Nashville, TN

Team: PPI Motorsports

Sponsor: Tide

Owner: Cal Wells III

Crew Chief: Harold Holly

Car: Chevrolet

Like father, like son: Hamilton Jr. continues the family tradition of NASCAR driving.

Kevin HARVICK

Kevin Harvick's breakthrough opportunity in Winston Cup racing wasn't supposed to happen when it did. But the death of Dale Earnhardt on the final lap of the Daytona 500 on February 18, 2001 forced Harvick into the fray much earlier than car owner Richard Childress had planned.

Harvick had intended to run for the championship in NASCAR's Busch Series, but when the NEXTEL Cup drivers took the green flag for the second race of the year at Rockingham, Harvick was behind the wheel of Childress' No. 29 Chevrolet. (In deference to Earnhardt, the No. 3 was retired indefinitely).

Thus began one of the most remarkable seasons in the history of stock car racing. Harvick went to Victory Lane in his third Winston Cup start, in a photo finish over Jeff Gordon at Atlanta Motor Speedway. Other than Jamie McMurray, who won in his second career start in 2002, no other driver in the modern era (1972 to date) has posted a win that soon after his debut.

Harvick wasn't finished. He won the inaugural NEXTEL Cup race at Chicagoland Speedway and ended the season ninth in the points standings, despite his absence from the Daytona 500. The next highest finish by a driver who did not run all 36 races was 25th (Robert Pressley).

And by the way, Harvick still managed to compete in the Busch Series, despite a schedule that often forced him to fly back and forth between races when Busch and NEXTEL Cup did not hold companion events. Despite the problems inherent in qualifying and practicing cars in two different series, Harvick nevertheless was strong enough to win the Busch title, backing up his rookie-of-the-year performance of 2000.

All told, counting one start in the Craftsman Truck Series, Harvick competed in 70 events at 30 different racetracks. In all of his racing endeavors combined, he covered more than 20,000 miles. Sweetening his remarkable rookie season was prize money totaling more than $4.3 million.

And it was Harvick's relationship with Childress that helped carry both owner and driver through a difficult season.

"Richard has done a lot for me in my career," Harvick said. "Basically, I was struggling in the Craftsman Truck Series to make a name for myself. Richard came out of nowhere and put me in his car in the Busch Series, and obviously when everything happened, I told him, 'You do whatever think is right, and I'm going to stand you behind you 100 percent.' That's what he did for me. It's not like going to a job where you go and say, 'Well, this is not in my contract,' because the fact of the matter is, we didn't even have a contract, and that didn't matter. I told him, 'We can do whatever it takes to make it all happen.'"

Though Harvick's ability to adapt to a NEXTEL Cup car seemed uncanny, those who had followed his career—including Childress—were not unduly surprised by his success. A Go-Kart racer since age 5, Harvick won seven national karting titles and two Grand National championships before climbing behind the wheel of a late model stock car. In 1993, at 18, he won the track championship at Mesa Marin Raceway in Bakersfield, California, his home town.

Harvick's fast track to NEXTEL Cup included a rookie-of-the-year crown in the Featherlite Southwest Series (1995), a Winston West championship (1998) and 11 top-10 finishes in his first season in the Truck Series (1999).

And lest we forget, 2001 was a banner year for Harvick in another sense—he married wife DeLana in Las Vegas two days after his Winston Cup debut at Rockingham.

Kevin Harvick won the Atlanta race in March of 2001 in his third Winston Cup start.

29

Birthdate: December 8, 1975

Birthplace: Bakersfield, CA

Team: Richard Childress Racing

Sponsor: GM Goodwrench

Owner: Richard Childress

Crew Chief: Todd Berrier

Car Make: Chevrolet

Kevin **HARVICK**

The promise of the rookie season, however, wasn't fulfilled by his performance in 2002, when Harvick slipped to 21st in points despite reprising his victory at Chicagoland. There were issues with his temper, which Harvick on occasion failed to control both on and off the track. The 2003 season appeared to be a turnaround, however. Harvick won the prestigious Brickyard 400, finished second six times and ended up fifth in points.

> ## I told him, 'We can do whatever it takes to make it all happen'.

But Harvick's uneven results continued in 2004, when he narrowly failed to qualify for the Chase for the NEXTEL Cup. Harvick was eighth in points two races before the cutoff, but a 28th-place finish at California knocked him out of the top 10 and out of the championship picture.

Harvick, though, is a magnificent talent and should be a contender for the championship for many years.

Kevin Harvick grabbed his NASCAR chance with both hands.

STATS (SINCE 2000)

YEAR	STARTS	WINS	TOP 5	TOP 10	MONEY
2000	did not compete				
2001	35	2	6	16	$4,302,202
2002	35	1	5	8	$3,849,216
2003	36	1	11	18	$6,237,119
2004	36	0	5	14	$4,718,562
CAREER	142	4	27	55	$19,107,099

Dale JARRETT

If the current roster of NASCAR superstars is heavily populated with "child prodigies"—Jeff Gordon, Tony Stewart and Kevin Harvick come to mind—you can count second-generation driver Dale Jarrett among the late bloomers, a somewhat surprising turn of events considering his pedigree.

The son of two-time Winston Cup champion Ned Jarrett, Dale didn't settle on a racing career during his teenage years, as had been the case with other notable sons of famous fathers (Richard and Kyle Petty, for instance). Instead, Jarrett played football, basketball and golf at Newton-Conover High School near his home town of Hickory, North Carolina—and he played them all extremely well. Jarrett was all-conference in all three sports and was accomplished enough at golf to consider a career as a professional. The University of South Carolina offered him full golf scholarship, which Jarrett declined.

The lure of racing finally overshadowed his affinity for other sports after Jarrett began driving limited sportsman cars at historic Hickory Motor Speedway in 1977, at age 20. He continued to make a name for himself in late model stocks until NASCAR revamped its Late Model Sportsman division as the Busch Series in 1982.

But success in the Busch Series (11 victories and 14 poles to his credit) didn't translate immediately to NEXTEL Cup. Jarrett's early years in NASCAR's elite series were almost pedestrian—he might as well have been walking. Driving sporadically for eight different car owners from 1984 through 1988—in equipment that was less than state-of-the-art—he failed to post a top-five finish in his first 57 starts.

After a 1989 season that produced two fifth-place finishes for owner Cale Yarborough, Jarrett signed on with the Wood Brothers in 1990. A year later, three months shy of his 35th birthday, Jarrett claimed his first NEXTEL Cup victory in the Champion 400 at Michigan.

The improved results of 1991 (two poles and a 17th-place finish in points to go with the win) provided the springboard Jarrett needed to land a ride with the rookie team of Joe Gibbs, the once-and-future coach of the Super Bowl champion Washington Redskins of the National Football League.

After a 1992 season that produced two top-fives and eight top-10s, Jarrett accounted for one of NASCAR's most unforgettable moments in the Daytona 500 of 1993. With his father calling the race from the television broadcast booth—and unable to contain his excitement—Jarrett edged Dale Earnhardt for the victory. Though he failed to win another race that season, Jarrett nevertheless posted 13 top-fives en route to his highest finish in the points thus far—fourth.

His third year with Gibbs was his last, but Jarrett did notch another victory in in the fall 1994 race at Charlotte. It was the following season, however, that would bring the association that would allow Jarrett to realize his full potential as a driver. With his regular driver, Ernie Irvan, unable to compete because of a career-threatening injury suffered during a practice crash at Michigan, car owner Robert Yates hired Jarrett to drive the No. 28 Ford in 1995. Jarrett won at Pocono, Pennsylvania, and finished third in points in his first season with Yates.

In 1996, Jarrett switched car numbers—to Yates' No. 88 Ford—and found a home. With crew chief Todd Parrott making the calls in the pits, Jarrett claimed four more victories, including his second Daytona 500 and the prestigious Brickyard 400 at Indianapolis. The following season

Dale Jarrett reached the pinnacle of his career with a Winston Cup championship in 1999.

Birthdate: November 28, 1956
Birthplace: Newton, NC
Team: Robert Yates Racing
Sponsor: UPS
Owner: Robert Yates
Crew Chief: Mike Ford
Car: Ford

Dale **JARRETT**

brought seven victories, a second-place finish in points and Jarrett's selection as Driver of the Year by the National Motorsports Press Association.

But 1999 was the pinnacle of Jarrett's career. He won four races on the way to his first NEXTEL Cup championship, at age 42. In doing so, Dale and Ned Jarrett became only the second father-son combination to win the series title, following Lee and Richard Petty.

The competition is closer, and that keeps your adrenaline going...

Jarrett backed up his championship season with two wins in 2000 and four more in 2001.

Though his 45th birthday is behind him, Jarrett doesn't see retirement in his immediate future. "I can only look back to Dale Earnhardt," Jarrett said. "He was still winning and very competitive [at age 49] and may have been on the verge of having another one of his better years before he was taken from us. I think that guys now are in better shape. Obviously, the competition is closer, and that keeps your adrenaline going a little bit." Jarrett hasn't matched his 1999 performance in the five years that have passed since his championship, and he narrowly missed qualifying for the inaugural Chase for the NEXTEL Cup in 2004. But Jarrett has one factor on his side—he seems to get better with age.

Dale Jarrett remains competitive as he heads towards 50.

STATS (SINCE 2000)

YEAR	STARTS	WINS	TOP 5	TOP 10	MONEY
2000	34	2	15	24	$5,934,475
2001	36	4	12	19	$5,377,742
2002	36	2	10	18	$4,421,951
2003	36	1	1	7	$4,121,187
2004	36	0	6	14	$4,539,330
CAREER	567	31	158	249	$46,357,600

Jimmie JOHNSON

A relative late-comer to stock car racing after gaining a wealth of "off-road" experience, Jimmie Johnson turned out to be the early bird when it came to advancing his NEXTEL Cup career.

In his first full season in the Busch Series (2000), Johnson turned the heads of several NEXTEL Cup owners with a 10th-place finish in the points. With a variety of opportunities opening up for him, Johnson went to Jeff Gordon for career advice in August of that year.

As it turned out, Gordon and Rick Hendrick had decided to start a fourth racing team, with Gordon as co-owner. Johnson was one of a handful of drivers they were considering, but Johnson's conversation with Gordon accelerated the process.

"To my surprise, he was interested and Rick Hendrick was interested in trying a fourth team, and all of a sudden, they're looking at me as being their driver," Johnson said. "…I think probably in a few months' to six months' time, they would have approached me… When I came to them with my situation, it kind of sped up the process, and it just made it all happen sooner. I think I would have been approached eventually, but it was destiny when I went to them as early as I did, and they reacted as they did."

Before he got his first taste of the Busch Series in 1998, Johnson was far more comfortable driving a truck on any surface other than asphalt. For three straight years, 1992–1994, he won the Mickey Thompson Stadium championship. In 1994, he also won the SCORE Desert Championship, and in 1996 and 1997 he claimed the SODA Winter Series title. In 1998, the same year he entered his first three Busch races, he also won Rookie of

the Year honors in the ASA ACDelco Challenge Series.

It wasn't until 2001 that Johnson won his first Busch Series race, the inaugural event at Chicagoland Speedway. With nine top-10 results that season, he finished eighth in points. Johnson also competed in three NEXTEL Cup races in 2001; in his debut at Charlotte he qualified 15th—a clear portent of strong efforts to come.

The start to his 2002 NEXTEL Cup rookie season couldn't have been better. Driving for Hendrick and Gordon, Johnson won the pole for the season-opening Daytona 500.

Johnson went on to win three races in 2002 and finished fifth in points. In 2003 he improved to second in the final standings. Johnson's flirtation with the NEXTEL Cup title continued in 2004 when the young driver finished second to Kurt Busch in the Chase for the NEXTEL Cup. Johnson won four of the season's final six races but came up one position short at Homestead and lost the championship by eight points.

STATS (SINCE 2000)

YEAR	STARTS	WINS	TOP 5	TOP 10	MONEY
2000	did not compete				
2001	3	0	0	0	$122,320
2002	36	3	6	21	$3,788,268
2003	36	3	14	20	$7,745,530
2004	36	8	19	22	$5,692,620
CAREER	**111**	**14**	**39**	**63**	**$17,348,738**

48

Birthdate: Sept. 17, 1975
Birthplace: El Cajon, CA
Team: Hendrick Motorsports
Sponsor: Lowe's
Owner: Rick Hendrick, Jeff Gordon
Crew Chief: Chad Knaus
Car: Chevrolet

Jimmie Johnson came close second in 2004's NEXTEL Cup Chase.

Kasey KAHNE

Kasey Kahne's first victory in NEXTEL Cup—when it finally comes—almost surely will open the floodgates for the 24-year-old driver. It's difficult to argue the point that Kahne used up most of his bad luck in 2004.

Most rookie drivers would take the rookie season Kahne had in 2004 and go home for the off-season in a state of euphoria. Collectively, five second-place finishes constitute a phenomenal performance for a first-year Cup driver. And winning Rookie of the Year honors should be enough to satisfy a neophyte. For Kahne, however, it was a frustrating year, because he came so tantalizingly close to victory and because he narrowly missed qualifying for the Chase for the NEXTEL Cup.

When car owner Ray Evernham announced in December of 2003 that Kahne would replace veteran Bill Elliott in the No. 9 Dodge, the decision raised eyebrows. Elliott, who was stepping back to a limited schedule in 2004, is one of the most talented—and popular—drivers ever to get behind the wheel of a stock car. Kahne, on the other hand, was unproven. With only one full season of Busch Series racing to his credit, and only one victory in the series, Kahne was an unlikely successor to a star of Elliott's magnitude.

The choice, though, speaks volumes about Evernham's eye for talent. Remember, it was Evernham who had guided Jeff Gordon to the first three of his four championships, and in Kahne, he saw similar potential. After a blown engine relegated the No. 9 Dodge to a disappointing 42nd-place finish in the season-opening Daytona 500, Kahne quickly began to validate the merit of Evernham's choice.

In the second race of 2004, at Rockingham, Kahne started third and finished second. The following week at

STATS (SINCE 2000)					
YEAR	STARTS	WINS	TOP 5	TOP 10	MONEY
2000		did not compete			
2001		did not compete			
2002		did not compete			
2003		did not compete			
2004	36	0	13	4	$4,759,002
CAREER	**36**	**0**	**13**	**4**	**$4,759,002**

Las Vegas he started from the pole, led 43 laps and came home second again. A week later, at Atlanta, Kane finished third, and the same voices that had questioned Evernham's selection of the young driver suddenly were declaring that the rookie's first NEXTEL Cup victory was imminent.

They were wrong. Kahne had the dominant car at Texas and led 148 laps—but finished second again. At Michigan he improved from a 34th-place starting position to second once more. He was third at Pocono, fourth at the Brickyard and fifth when the series visited Michigan for a second time.

Kahne was second in the Labor Day weekend race at California. At Charlotte in October, he again had the dominant car and led 207 laps, but a late-race accident resulting from tire failure deprived him of victory.

As disappointing as the rash of seconds was Kahne's failure to qualify for the Chase for the NEXTEL Cup. One week before the cut-off, the 26th race of the season at Richmond, he was ninth in points, but a 24th-place result knocked him out of the top 10.

But Kahne should remember that it took him two years to claim his first win in the Busch Series—and 2005 will be his second year in Cup. When he finally does taste victory, it will likely be the appetizer in a seven-course dinner.

Although Kahne didn't make the Chase for the NEXTEL Cup in 2004, he's sure to be back for more.

9

Birthdate: April 10, 1980

Birthplace: Enumclaw, WA

Team: Evernham Motorsports

Sponsor: Dodge Dealers/UAW

Owner: Ray Evernham

Crew Chief: Tommy Baldwin

Car: Dodge

Matt KENSETH

Perhaps the greatest compliment to a teacher is for a student to surpass his mentor's level of accomplishment. In 2003, when he won the NEXTEL Cup title, Matt Kenseth did just that.

NEXTEL Cup veteran Mark Martin first took notice of Kenseth's formidable talent during a Busch Series race at Talladega, Alabama. Since then, the two drivers have enjoyed a solid friendship born of mutual respect. Martin helped teach Kenseth the nuances of big-time stock car racing, and Kenseth quickly became a big-time star in his own right.

It was no surprise that Kenseth's name would rise to the top of the list in 1999, when owner Jack Roush (who has fielded cars for Martin since 1988) wanted to expand his operation. And it wasn't simply that Martin lobbied earnestly on his young friend's behalf.

Kenseth had already shown his mettle in 1998 as a substitute driver for Bill Elliott, who missed a race while attending his father's funeral. Kenseth drove Elliott's No. 94 Ford to a sixth-place finish at the difficult "Monster Mile" in Dover, Delaware, a remarkable accomplishment for his first "seat time" in a NEXTEL Cup car.

A full-time competitor in the Busch Series in 1999, Kenseth also competed in five Cup events for Roush, and Dover was again the high-water mark of the season. Kenseth posted a fourth-place finish there, his first career top-five in NASCAR's top series.

In 2000, his first full season of NEXTEL Cup racing, Kenseth won the series' longest race, the Coca-Cola 600 at Charlotte. He also won Rookie of the Year honors—a victory that wasn't entirely popular in some quarters, given that the taciturn Kenseth edged out the flamboyant and charismatic Dale Earnhardt Jr. for the rookie crown.

STATS (SINCE 2000)

YEAR	STARTS	WINS	TOP 5	TOP 10	MONEY
2000	34	1	4	11	$2,408,138
2001	36	0	4	9	$2,565,579
2002	36	5	11	19	$4,514,203
2003	36	1	11	25	$9,422,786
2004	36	2	8	16	$6,223,892
CAREER	**184**	**9**	**39**	**82**	**$25,320,477**

But it should be no knock against Kenseth that he is a business on the track. During his rookie season, he finishe 10th in the season-opening Daytona 500 and went on t record 10 more top-10s before the end of the campaign. was that level of consistency that allowed him to stay ahea of Earnhardt Jr. in the rookie standings. Overall, Kenset finished 14th in points.

He improved one position in 2001, a year in which th entire Roush organization lost ground to the rest of the to teams. Nevertheless, Kenseth posted nine top-10s an earned $2,565,579 in prize money. He had three fourth place finishes—at Michigan, Talladega and Phoenix—bu nothing better. Early in 2002, however, Kenseth found cure for his winless season of 2001. In February, he won th Pop Secret 400 at Rockingham, the same track where h notched his first Busch Series victory in 1998 in a last-la shootout with Tony Stewart.

That was the first of five 2002 victories for the Wisconsi native. Though Kenseth won only once in 2003, his 11 top fives and 25 top-10s were enough to propel him to the serie championship. Kenseth also picked up a pair of wins i 2004 and qualified for the first Chase for the NEXTEL Cup but a series of mishaps in the final 10 races relegated him t an eighth-place points finish. Don't believe for a momen however, that Kenseth won't make another strong title rur

Birthdate: March 10, 1972

Birthplace: Cambridge, WI

Team: Roush Racing

Sponsor: DeWalt Power Tools

Owner: Jack Roush

Crew Chief: Robbie Reiser

Car: Ford

Matt Kenseth celebrates victory at Rockingham

Bobby LABONTE

Which "brother act" is the most successful in the history of Winston Cup racing? You could argue the point, because there are many famous names that could deserve the accolade.

You could make a case for Tim, Fonty and Bob Flock, who totalled 63 victories between them in the early days of NASCAR.

Bobby and Donnie Allison could lay a strong claim to that distinction. Bobby himself accounted for 84 wins and a championship in 1983, while Donnie added 10 victories to the family record book. On four occasions when Donnie took the checkered flag, Bobby was right behind in second place.

But Bobby Labonte's NEXTEL Cup championship in 2000 was unprecedented—with that title, he and brother Terry Labonte (a two-time champion) became the only pair of brothers ever to win NASCAR's most coveted prize.

Bobby Labonte was a quick study. When brother Terry was driving for Billy Hagan during the mid-1980s, Bobby was a member of the crew. Together they celebrated Terry's first NEXTELCup championship in 1984.

In 1987, Bobby took a job with car builder Jay Hedgecock. On the weekends he raced late model stock cars at Caraway Speedway in Asheboro, North Carolina. Working on his own cars, he won 12 races and the track title in 1987.

Gradually, Labonte worked his way into the Busch Series. In 1990 he ran the full Busch Grand National schedule for the first time and finished fourth in the points race. A year later he won the Busch title.

The 1991 season also marked Labonte's first foray into NEXTEL Cup racing—he competed in two events in his own car and failed to finish either one. The $8,350 he won

for those first two starts was a far cry from the millions that awaited him later in the decade.

Labonte was absent from NEXTEL Cup in 1992, when he finished three points behind Joe Nemechek in the closest contest for the Busch championship in series history—after he and Todd Bodine rescued Nemechek from a burning car during the season-opening race at Daytona.

When he returned to NASCAR's top series in 1993, Labonte ran a full schedule for owner Bill Davis. Though winless in two seasons for Davis, Labonte claimed his first NEXTEL Cup pole position in the fall 1993 race at Richmond, Virginia.

In 1995 Labonte began the association with owner Joe Gibbs that eventually would lead to the championship in 2000. In each of his first eight seasons with Gibbs, since taking over the No. 18 Interstate Batteries car from Dale Jarrett, Labonte won at least one race and accumulated 18 career victories by the end of 2001. Though eight years younger than Terry, who was born in 1956—and though he made his NEXTEL Cup debut 13 years after Terry's in 1978—Bobby is closing fast on his brother's total of 21 wins through 2001.

Labonte's most prolific year in terms of visits to Victory Lane was 1999, when he finished second in the title race to Dale Jarrett. Labonte won five times that season—at Dover, at Pocono twice, at Michigan and at Atlanta. During his championship season a year later, he cemented his claim to the title with an early win at Rockingham, his first victory in the Brickyard 400 at Indianapolis, his first victory in the Southern 500 at Darlington, and an emphatic win in the October race at Charlotte.

As is often the case after the euphoria of a championship season, Labonte's defense of his title got off to an extremely slow start. Seven races into the 2001 season, he

Bobby Labonte drove the No. 18 Pontiac to the Winston Cup championship in 2000.

18

Birthdate: May 8, 1964

Birthplace: Corpus Christi, TX

Team: Joe Gibbs Racing

Sponsor: Interstate Batteries

Owner: Joe Gibbs

Crew Chief: Brandon Thomas

Car: Chevrolet

stood 25th in points, but Labonte rallied during the latter portion of the year to finish sixth. He posted two victories after the season's midpoint at two of his favorite tracks— Pocono and Atlanta.

Labonte was quick to share credit for his success with crew chief Jimmy Makar, who has called the shots in the pits during each of Labonte's seasons with Gibbs.

"I've never seen a more determined man about racing,"

...whenever he decides to quit, I'm going to quit, too.

Labonte said at the time. "Our relationship goes back a long way, and we've become great friends over the past years, and we've kind of set up that whenever he decides to quit, I'm going to quit, too."

It didn't quite work out that way. After a 16th-place finish in 2002, Makar took on the general manager's role at Joe Gibbs Racing, and Michael "Fatback" McSwain assumed the crew chief duties for the No. 18 team. The tumultuous relationship between the driver and the new pit boss didn't last. In 2004 McSwain departed for the Wood Brothers team and driver Ricky Rudd, and Labonte fell from ninth to 13th in the final two races that determined eligibility for the Chase for the NEXTEL Cup.

Bobby Labonte's outstanding talent has seen him earn close on $40 million; he has earned more even than his brother Terry.

STATS (SINCE 2000)

YEAR	STARTS	WINS	TOP 5	TOP 10	MONEY
2000	34	4	19	24	$7,361,386
2001	36	2	9	20	$4,786,779
2002	36	1	5	7	$4,183,715
2003	36	2	12	17	$5,505,018
2004	36	0	5	11	$4,570,545
CAREER	**402**	**21**	**106**	**177**	**$40,212,302**

Terry LABONTE

"Texas" Terry Labonte is known as the Iron Man of NEXTEL Cup racing for a good reason. His 655 consecutive starts, spanning more than 20 years, constitute a series record that's in no danger of being broken any time soon.

And it's not that Labonte simply "turned laps" in those 655 races, before his streak was broken at Indianapolis in 2000. His career has included 22 victories, 27 poles and a pair of championships.

Labonte got an early start on his lengthy career. At age seven, he began racing quarter midgets in his native Texas. In 1978, as an unheralded 21-year-old, he landed a ride with car owner Billy Hagan for the Southern 500 at Darlington. Winston Cup veterans were surprised when Labonte qualified 19th for the prestigious race. When he drove Hagan's Chevrolet to a fourth-place finish, they were dumbfounded.

Labonte won $9,850 for his remarkable showing that Sunday. By the end of 2001, his career earnings had exceeded $25 million.

The 1978 Southern 500 began an association with Hagan that lasted nine years. Never a prolific winner on the NEXTEL Cup circuit, Labonte posted his first victory in the 1980 Southern 500 at Darlington, appropriately enough. All told, he won six races for Hagan before signing with Junior Johnson for the 1987 season.

Labonte's tenure with Hagan also included the first of his series titles, in 1984. Though he won but two races that season, at Riverside, California, and Bristol, Tennessee, Labonte was the model of consistency. He had six seconds and six thirds to go with the two victories.

Labonte won four races for Johnson before changing owners again in 1990. Winless with Richard Jackson that season, Labonte returned to Hagan in 1991, but the drought

STATS (SINCE 2000)

YEAR	STARTS	WINS	TOP 5	TOP 10	MONEY
2000	32	0	3	6	$2,475,365
2001	36	0	1	3	$3,011,911
2002	36	0	1	4	$3,244,240
2003	36	1	4	9	$4,283,625
2004	36	0	0	6	$3,745,242
CAREER	**817**	**22**	**181**	**359**	**$37,809,799**

continued for three years. It wasn't until Labonte accepte a ride from Rick Hendrick in 1994 that his fortunes took turn for the better.

He won three times that season, at now-defunct Nor Wilkesboro, Richmond and Phoenix. A year later I matched that career-best mark for victories in a season wi wins at Richmond, Pocono and Bristol.

The third season with Hendrick brought two victories and a second championship. The 12-year span between th first and second titles is a record for the NEXTEL Cu Series. It was also in 1996 that Labonte eclipsed Richa Petty's record 514 consecutive starts.

Three-and-a-half years later, injuries suffered in violent crash in the Pepsi 400 at Daytona forced Labonte miss the Brickyard 400, and the streak ended at 655 race For the first year since 1993, and the first since he joine Hendrick Motorsports, Labonte failed to win a race.

The drought lasted until 2003, when Labonte won th Southern 500 for the second time, 23 years after his fir victory at Darlington. In October of 2004, the Iron Ma announced that he would turn over the No. 5 Chevrolet Brian Vickers in 2005, when Labonte himself planned to ru a limited schedule.

5

Birthdate: November 16, 1956
Birthplace: Corpus Christi, TX
Team: Hendrick Motorsports
Sponsor: Kellogg's
Owner: Rick Hendrick
Crew Chief: Peter Sospenzo
Car Make: Chevrolet

Texas Terry Labonte is the "Iron Man" of NEXTEL Cup racin

Sterling **MARLIN**

If ever a driver defied conventional wisdom in 2001 and 2002, that driver was Sterling Marlin. In fact, Marlin was on the verge of a championship in 2002— until fate intervened.

Bill Elliott and Casey Atwood were supposed to be at the vanguard of Dodge's triumphant return to NEXTEL Cup racing in 2001, in cars fielded by Ray Evernham with the backing and blessing of the Chrysler Corporation.

But it was Marlin, a restrictor-plate racing specialist, who led the parade, driving for a team revitalized by the advent of vaunted IndyCar owner Chip Ganassi, who had purchased a controlling interest in Felix Sabates' SABCO organization.

With Ganassi at the helm, Marlin ended four years of famine with a victory at Michigan in August—the first win for a Dodge since the late Neil Bonnett took the checkered flag at Ontario, California, on Nov. 20, 1977. Marlin followed with a victory in the October race at Charlotte, and his third-place finish in the championship standings was the best among the Dodge drivers in 2001. With more than $4.5 million in prize money, Marlin more than doubled his previous best season in the earnings category ($2.253 million in 1995). His 12 top-five finishes were a testament to the quality of the Ganassi organization.

The son of former NEXTEL Cup driver Coo Coo Marlin, Sterling got his start in the series in 1976 at Nashville Raceway, his home track. Substituting for his father, who was sidelined with a broken shoulder, Marlin failed to finish the race.

All told, in a career that has spanned more than a quarter-century, Marlin has driven NEXTEL Cup cars for 16 different owners. His first full season on the circuit didn't come until 1983, when he won Rookie of the Year honors driving for Roger Hamby—though he posted just one top-10 result in 30 races.

It took Marlin eight more years to win his first pole—in a car fielded by Junior Johnson. In 1992 he won five poles, starting in front for both Daytona races and the second event at Talladega, thereby establishing himself as a contender on NASCAR's two restrictor-plate superspeedways.

It wasn't until 1994, however, that Marlin won his first race—appropriately enough, the season-opening Daytona 500. That was his first appearance with the Morgan-McClure Racing team, whose prowess at building restrictor-plate engines meshed perfectly with Marlin's ability to drive the cars.

The Daytona 500 gave Marlin his only victory of 1994, but as if to prove it was no accident, he repeated the feat the following year and joined Richard Petty (1973–74) and Cale Yarborough (1983–84) as the only drivers to win NASCAR's most important race in consecutive years. Marlin's third-place finish in the 1995 points standings also was a career-best. Before the season was over, he added victories at Darlington and Talladega to his Daytona 500 win.

Before leaving Morgan-McClure after the 1997 season, Marlin won twice more—in the 1996 Pepsi 400 at Daytona and the 1996 Talladega 500. The three years that followed his departure must have seemed like Purgatory to the veteran driver. With Sabates, Marlin posted just three top-fives in three seasons, and his best finish in the points was 13th in 1998.

Enter Ganassi and the new alliance with Dodge. That was all Marlin needed to jump-start his career.

"I think the last few races (of 2001) showed how good

Birthdate: June 30, 1957

Birthplace: Columbia, TN

Team: Chip Ganassi Racing with Felix Sabates

Sponsor: Coors Light

Owner: Chip Ganassi, Felix Sabates

Crew Chief: Tony Glover

Car: Dodge

Sterling Marlin gets some last-minute advice before firing the engine in his No. 40 Dodge.

we really were," Marlin said. "Chip turned this team around and reorganized the whole place. He hired a lot more people, had Ernie Elliott [Bill Elliott's brother] build our motors, and everything just went real smooth."

It was smooth sailing for Marlin in 2002, when he led the points standings for 25 straight races and appeared headed for the NEXTEL Cup title. But a broken vertebra in his neck, the result of successive violent crashes at Richmond and Kansas City, ended his season on September 29, and Marlin fell to 18th in points.

Was the 2002 season Marlin's last, best chance for a championship? That remains to be seen, but at age 46,

I think the last few races [of 2001] showed how good we really were.

Marlin failed to win a race in 2003 and finished 18th in points. In 2004 he was winless and 19th in points at the cutoff for the Chase for the NEXTEL Cup.

Then again, based on his unexpected performances 2001 and 2002, perhaps Marlin has a few surprises left.

Sparks fly from Sterling Marlin's Dodge.

STATS (SINCE 2000)

YEAR	STARTS	WINS	TOP 5	TOP 10	MONEY
2000	34	0	1	7	$1,992,301
2001	36	2	12	20	$4,517,634
2002	29	2	8	14	$4,228,889
2003	36	0	0	11	$4,384,941
2004	36	0	3	7	$4,057,753
CAREER	640	10	82	210	$32,570,672

Jamie McMURRAY

The question for Jamie McMurray is not "When will you win your first race?"

but "When will you win your second one?"

McMurray answered the former question quicker than any other driver in the modern history of NEXTEL Cup. In his second career start in October of 2002, substituting for injured Sterling Marlin at Lowe's Motor Speedway in Charlotte, McMurray outran the competition and claimed a startling victory.

The disclaimer was that McMurray was driving a championship-caliber car, one that had the led the points standings for 25 weeks before Marlin was sidelined with a cracked vertebra in his neck. But McMurray brought the No. 40 Coors Light Dodge to the checkered flag unscathed and demonstrated beyond question his ability to win.

Fast forward two years. McMurray is the full-time driver of Chip Ganassi's No. 42 Havoline Dodge, but he has yet to visit Victory Lane in his own ride. To be sure, he's had his chances. In 2003 McMurray was third twice, at Bristol and at Indianapolis. In 2004 he was again third at the last NEXTEL Cup race scheduled for North Carolina Speedway in Rockingham.

He ran second at Infineon Raceway's road course in Sonoma, California, and late in the 2004 season he put together a string of six straight top-10 finishes as he sought to qualify for the Chase for the NEXTEL Cup. To McMurray's chagrin, he finished the 26th race of the season 11th in points, one rung away from the Chase.

Given the depth of his talent, it's not a question of whether McMurray will win again. It's a question of when. Remember that the young gun from Joplin, Missouri won his first two Busch Series races and the Cup race at Charlotte within a four-week period, making him stock car

racing's version of "Mr. October." And remember that, at the time, McMurray was just 26 years old.

He was 8 when he started racing go-karts, and by 199[ ] he had won four U.S. Go-Kart titles. From a World Kartin[g] championship in 1991 McMurray progressed to a trac[k] championship in late model stock cars at I-44 Speedway i[n] 1997. In 1999 he competed in five races in NASCAR[ ] Craftsman Truck Series before running a full schedule i[n] 2000, the same year he made his debut in the Busch Serie[s] in a car owned by Clarence Brewer.

McMurray was third in Busch Rookie of the Year poin[ts] in 2001, when he competed in a full slate of races for th[e] first time. Then came the watershed events of 2002, whe[n] McMurray finished sixth in the final Busch Series standing[s] in addition to winning his second NEXTEL Cup start.

Ganassi had already hired McMurray to compete i[n] NEXTEL Cup in 2003 before the serendipitous victory a[t] Charlotte, but that win only reinforced Ganassi's confiden[ce] in the young driver's ability to handle a high-tech stock ca[r.]

True enough, McMurray hasn't won a race in more tha[n] two years, but in 2004 he failed to qualify for the Chase fo[r] the NEXTEL Cup by a razor-thin margin. He was 11th i[n] points at the line of demarcation after 26 races.

Chances are, however, that McMurray won't have [to] wait too much longer for his next victory, not to mention [a] possible series championship.

McMurray missed out on the NEXTEL Cup chase by one plac[e]

STATS (SINCE 2000)

YEAR	STARTS	WINS	TOP 5	TOP 10	MONEY
2000	did not compete				
2001	did not compete				
2002	6	1	1	2	$717,942
2003	36	0	5	13	$3,258,806
2004	36	0	9	23	$3,636,311
CAREER	**78**	**1**	**15**	**38**	**$7,613,059**

42

Birthdate: June 3, 1976

Birthplace: Joplin, MO

Team: Chip Ganassi Racing with Felix Sabates

Sponsor: Texaco/Havoline

Owner: Chip Ganassi, Felix Sabates

Crew Chief: Donnie Wingo

Car: Dodge

Mark MARTIN

Having announced his impending retirement after the 2005 season, Mark Martin has enjoyed a NASCAR career that places him among the all-time greats of the sport.

Consider that Martin entered the 2005 season with 34 career NEXTEL Cup victories, 17th on the all-time list. Consider that Martin has won races on every sort of venue—from the shorts tracks at Richmond, North Wilkesboro and Martinsville to the intermediate speedways at Charlotte and Atlanta to the high banks of Talladega to the road courses at Sears Point (California) and Watkins Glen (New York).

Consider that Martin shattered the record for victories in the Busch Series (he has won 45 races) while competing almost exclusively in companion events that coincided with his NEXTEL Cup schedule.

Consider that Martin won a career-best seven Cup events in 1998, and that from 1989 through 2000, he never finished outside the top 10 in the NEXTEL Cup standings.

There is, however, one significant accomplishment Martin would like to add to his resume before he leaves the sport: a NEXTEL Cup championship, and the 2005 season represents his last opportunity.

Martin has come tantalizingly close to realizing that dream—never more so than in 1990, when he finished second in the standings, 26 points behind the late Dale Earnhardt. But for a 46-point penalty for a carburetor infraction discovered after Martin's victory at Richmond in February, he might well have won the title that year.

In 1997 Martin was third in the championship race, a mere 29 points behind winner Jeff Gordon, and in 1998 he was a distant second to Gordon—ever the bridesmaid.

STATS (SINCE 2000)

YEAR	STARTS	WINS	TOP 5	TOP 10	MONEY
2000	34	1	13	20	$3,098,874
2001	36	0	13	20	$3,797,006
2002	36	1	12	22	$7,004,893
2003	36	0	5	10	$4,486,560
2004	36	1	10	15	$3,948,497
CAREER	602	34	215	340	$44,605,472

In 2004 he entered the final race in the Chase for the NEXTEL Cup with an outside chance to win the championship but finished fourth in the standings.

Despite the lack of a title, however, Martin is an Arkansas boy who has arrived in the big-time. But his success didn't come quickly. He started 57 races for seven different owners (including himself), before making the deal that would propel him into the upper echelons of stock car racing. In 1988, he signed on with Jack Roush. The association is one of uncharacteristic loyalty on both sides. Despite a disappointing 2001, when he failed to win a race for the first time since 1996; despite back problems that have necessitated surgery and limited Martin's ability to pursue daily workouts in the gym; despite rumblings that the Roush teams were on the decline, Martin and Roush began their 15th season together in 2002.

The irony is that another Roush driver, Matt Kenseth, brought the owner his first NEXTEL Cup title in 2003, and another Martin stable mate, Kurt Busch, won the Chase for the Championship in 2004. Though Martin can enjoy his teammates' success vicariously, he'd rather have a crown of his own. Accordingly, the 2005 season promises a scintillating performance from the talented veteran.

Mark Martin has won 32 Winston Cup races since joining forces with Jack Roush in 1988.

6

Birthdate: January 9, 1959
Birthplace: Batesville, AR
Team: Roush Racing
Sponsor: Viagra
Owner: Jack Roush
Crew Chief: Pat Tryson
Car: Ford

Jeremy **MAYFIELD**

No one has ever claimed that Jeremy Mayfield lacks self-assurance. Admirers might call him confident. Detractors might characterize his manner as downright cocky.

Whatever the label, the brash 35-year-old driver from Kentucky has ample reason to believe in his own abilities. So does car owner Ray Evernham, who brought Mayfield into his flagship Dodge organization before the start of the 2002 season.

Though Mayfield had just three victories to his credit in nine years on the Winston Cup circuit, Evernham thought enough of the young driver to put him behind the wheel of the No. 19 Dodge. Two seasons later, Mayfield vindicated Evernham's judgment by qualifying for the Chase for the NEXTEL Cup (with a victory in the 26th race of the season at Richmond) and finishing 10th in the final points standings.

A driver who developed his skills in late model stock cars and the touring ARCA Series, Mayfield made his NEXTEL Cup debut at Charlotte in October of 1993; he started 30th and finished 29th—10 laps down—in Earl Sadler's No. 95 Ford.

In 1994 he drove four times for Sadler, four times for T.W. Taylor and 12 times for former NEXTEL Cup champion Cale Yarborough. By his own admission, Yarborough did not have the finances to put top-quality equipment on the track, and Mayfield managed just two top-five results during his two-year tenure with the only driver to win three straight Winston Cup championships.

The 1996 season brought one of the most interesting "deals" in the history of NASCAR racing. Though it wasn't a "trade" in the same sense as a swap of baseball players, Mayfield and John Andretti switched rides two-thirds of the way through the year. Andretti left the Michael

STATS (SINCE 2000)					
YEAR	STARTS	WINS	TOP 5	TOP 10	MONEY
2000	32	2	6	12	$2,169,251
2001	28	0	5	7	$2,682,603
2002	36	0	2	4	$2,494,583
2003	36	0	4	12	$3,371,879
2004	36	1	5	13	$3,892,573
CAREER	**345**	**4**	**44**	**87**	**$21,488,248**

Kranefuss team to drive for Yarborough, and Mayfield signed on to drive for Kranefuss.

Though he failed to win in 1997, Mayfield improved his level of performance with three top-fives, eight top-10s and a 13th-place finish in the championship standings. Roger Penske bought into the team before the 1998 season, and coincidentally or not, Mayfield recorded his first victory in the June race at Pocono, Pennsylvania, and finished seventh in points.

After a winless 1999 season, Mayfield recorded two more wins during an inconsistent 2000 campaign. He won at Fontana, California, in April—on a two-mile super speedway owned by Penske—and followed that his second victory at Pocono, where he pulled the "bump-and-run" on the late Dale Earnhardt on the final lap.

"I was just trying to rattle his cage," Mayfield said of the final-lap incident, borrowing Earnhardt's own description of a similar situation between Earnhardt and Terry Labonte at Bristol in August of 1999.

Mayfield, however, failed to finish 11 races in 2000, and friction between Mayfield and teammate Rusty Wallace, the Penske organization's No. 1 driver, was an ill-kept secret. Twenty-eight races into the 2001 season, Mayfield was released by Penske and went off in pursuit of the ride he coveted. The announcement that he would join Evernham came before the end of the year.

"To have a guy like Ray Evernham on your side—who pushes you to be your best and then encourages to give

19

Birthdate: May 27, 1969

Birthplace: Owensboro, KY

Team: Evernham Motorsports

Sponsor: Dodge Dealers/UAW

Owner: Ray Evernham

Crew Chief: Ken Francis

Car: Dodge

Jeremy Mayfield has gone from Mobil 1 Ford to Dodge.

more—is what I've always wanted," Mayfield said. "He's a true racer in every sense of the word, and I respect him more than anybody.

"I never thought I would actually get to race for him. When he first put his deal together we talked, but I couldn't get out of my contract, and then he hired Casey (Atwood). I thought it was going to be too late. I thought I had lost my chance, but when Roger (Penske) let go of me the Monday night after Kansas City, Ray called me Tuesday morning and that was the best vote of confidence anyone could have given me."

Casey MEARS

Talk about a pedigree. Casey Mears has one. His father, Rogers Mears, is a former IndyCar driver and off-road champion.

His uncle is none other than four-time Indianapolis 500 winner Rick Mears. Given that background, Casey Mears might seem pre-ordained to compete at the highest levels of open-wheeled racing. For a time, in fact, that's precisely the direction he was headed.

In 1995, at age 17, Mears won the Jim Russell USAC Triple Crown championship. In 1999 he finished second in the Indy Lights series standings, having become the fourth driver to complete every lap during a single season of Indy Lights racing.

But 2001 brought a change of direction for the young driver, who competed in his first race in NASCAR's Busch Series. Driving a car owned by Wayne Jesel and Frank Cicci, Mears qualified 21st and finished 28th in his inaugural race at Homestead-Miami Speedway.

Three months later, Mears embarked on his first full season in the Busch Series. The highlights of 2002 were a third-place qualifying run at Las Vegas and a fifth-place finish in the April race at Talladega. At season's end, Mears was 21st in the Busch Series points standings.

Car owner Chip Ganassi nevertheless thought enough of Mears to hire him as the full-time driver of the No. 41 Target Dodge for the 2003 season. Never mind that Mears had only one top five in his Busch Series career. Ganassi has a discerning eye for driving talent, and the name "Mears" carries considerable weight, especially to an owner who has enjoyed success in both open-wheeled and stock car racing.

Despite the talent and the reputation, however, Mears suffered through a trying season in his first NEXTEL Cup campaign. Only three times in 2003 did he qualify in the top 10—with his best starting position a fourth a Chicago—and not once did he post a top-10 finish. In fact, a 15th-place result at Las Vegas in March was his best, and his final points position of 35th was among the lowest of those who competed in every race.

Though there was speculation in some quarters that Mears might lose his ride for 2004, Ganassi was steadfast in his support of the young driver, and early in the season, race fans began to see why. Mears finished seventh in the third race of the season, at Las Vegas, posting his first top 10 as a NEXTEL Cup driver. A week later at Atlanta he qualified ninth and led 37 laps before his motor expired with 23 laps remaining.

Four more top 10s followed the Las Vegas performance before Mears achieved his best NEXTEL Cup result to date, a fourth at the road course at Watkins Glen, New York. Over the next nine races, however, he finished in the top 10 only once and slipped from 16th to 20th in NEXTEL Cup points.

Nonetheless, Mears' sophomore season in NEXTEL Cup represented a dramatic improvement from his rookie year. If he continues to take giant steps, Mears will be a perennial contender for the championship.

STATS (SINCE 2000)

YEAR	STARTS	WINS	TOP 5	TOP 10	MONEY
2000	did not compete				
2001	did not compete				
2002	did not compete				
2003	36	0	0	0	$2,639,178
2004	36	0	1	9	$3,230,317
CAREER	**72**	**0**	**1**	**9**	**$5,869,495**

41

Birthdate: March 12, 1978
Birthplace: Bakersfield, CA
Team: Chip Ganassi Racing with Felix Sabates
Sponsor: Target Stores
Owner: Chip Ganassi, Felix Sabates
Crew Chief: Jimmy Elledge
Car: Dodge

Casey Mears made steady progress over the 2004 season, improving on 2003's disappointing debut.

Joe NEMECHEK

Nicknamed "Front Row Joe" for his prowess in qualifying sessions, Joe Nemechek may have finally found the right showcase for his formidable talents as a driver.

Nemechek had hoped 2002 was going to be the year. After winning the second race of his NEXTEL Cup career for owner Andy Petree at Rockingham in 2001, Nemechek signed with Carter-Haas Racing for 2002. At Carter-Haas, Nemechek was to team with long-time friend Todd Bodine, or so he thought.

The bankruptcy of the teams' primary sponsor, Kmart, threw the season into turmoil. Nemechek competed in only seven races for Carter-Haas, but the ill fortune of a fellow driver gave Nemechek another chance. He replaced injured Jerry Nadeau in the No. 25 Hendrick Motorsports Chevrolet for the final 25 races of the season.

Nemechek began the 2003 season with Hendrick but was released in favor of 2003 Busch Series champion Brian Vickers before the end of the year—despite posting a victory at Richmond. Nemechek finished the season in Nelson Bower's No. 01 U.S. Army-sponsored ride, and in 2004, still with Bowers, he won consecutive poles at Talladega and Kansas City. In the latter race, Nemechek finished where he started, notching his fourth career victory on October 10.

Nemechek made his NEXTEL Cup debut in 1993 at New Hampshire, the same track that would be the site of his first victory in 1999. After three races in his own car and two in a car owned by Morgan-McClure in 1993, Nemechek competed in his first full season of Cup racing for owner Larry Hedrick in 1994. In 1995 and 1996 he again ran a full schedule as an owner/driver. In three subsequent seasons with owner Felix Sabates, he claimed his first victory at

STATS (SINCE 2000)

YEAR	STARTS	WINS	TOP 5	TOP 10	MONEY
2000	34	0	3	9	$2,105,041
2001	31	1	1	4	$2,543,660
2002	33	0	3	3	$2,453,024
2003	36	1	2	6	$2,626,484
2004	36	1	3	9	$3,872,415
CAREER	**358**	**4**	**16**	**50**	**$18,854,530**

New Hampshire before signing with Petree for 2000.

Nemechek's difficulty getting to Victory Lane in the NEXTEL Cup series was a new and frustrating experience for the Florida-born driver. Unlike many fellow competitors who started racing Go-Karts, Nemechek got his first taste of competitive racing on a motorcycle at age 13.

Subsequently, he won Rookie of the Year honors and championships in three different racing divisions in three consecutive years: the Southeastern Mini-Stock Series (1987), the United Stock Car Alliance (1988) and NASCAR's All-Pro Series for late model stock cars (1989).

In 1990 Nemechek won the Rookie of the Year award in the Busch Series, and in 1992 he claimed the Busch championship. Throughout his NEXTEL Cup career, he has continued to race in a number of Busch Series events, none more dramatic than the season's final race at Homestead, Florida in 1997. Nemechek triumphed at the same track where his brother John had lost his life earlier that year.

In 190 Busch Series starts through 2001, Nemechek accumulated nine victories and ten pole positions. As the 2002 season approached, before Kmart's bankruptcy hit the news, Nemechek was optimistic about the move to Carter's team. Since then, he has driven for three different teams, including a one-race substitution for injured Johnny Benson in 2002. But as Nemechek has proven recently, all he needs is some stability to get to the front row—and stay there.

01

Birthdate: September 26, 1973

Birthplace: Lakeland, FL

Team: MB2 Motorsports

Sponsor: U.S. Army

Owner: Nelson Bowers

Crew Chief: Ryan Pemberton

Car: Chevrolet

Joe Nemechek and team celebrate his fourth career victory at Kansas City in 2004.

Ryan NEWMAN

Where did this guy come from? After 2004, his third full season in NEXTEL Cup racing, Newman had claimed 11 victories and an astonishing 27 pole positions—tied for 23rd on the all-time list with veteran Terry Labonte, whose career spans a quarter-century.

It almost seems unfair to the myriad drivers who have spent a lifetime chasing success in NASCAR's top series.

Ryan Newman has made an earlier, grander entrance to the sport than the two foremost open-wheeled prodigies who preceded him—Jeff Gordon and Tony Stewart. A virtuoso behind the steering wheel—like the young Mozart at the piano—Newman won the pole for the Coca-Cola 600 at Charlotte in 2001, in his third attempt to qualify for a NEXTEL Cup race. In doing so, he tied veteran Mark Martin for the earliest pole in a career.

Competing in seven races for owner Roger Penske in 2001, Newman posted a second-place finish at Kansas City and a fifth at Michigan. Though Newman was hardly a household word in stock car racing circles, that sort of immediate success surprised no one familiar with his career in USAC cars.

Already a member of the Quarter-Midget Hall of Fame, Newman is the only USAC driver ever to win Rookie of the Year honors in the Midget, Sprint and Silver Bullet series. In 1999, he won the Coors Light Silver Bullet national championship, and in the same year, he became the first driver to win at least one race in all three major USAC divisions: Silver Bullet, Midget and Sprint Cars.

In 2000, Newman made his stock car debut in an ARCA race in Michigan. In his second outing, he won—at Pocono, Pennsylvania. Before the season was over, he collected two more victories, at Kentucky Speedway and at Lowe's Motor Speedway in Charlotte.

Since then, Newman's rise to stardom has been meteoric. He won his first NEXTEL Cup race, at New Hampshire, in 2002 and followed that initial victory with eight wins and 11 poles in 2003.

In 2004, Newman visited Victory Lane twice, qualified for the Chase for the NEXTEL Cup and finished seventh in the final points standings.

Coincidentally, both Newman and his crew chief, Matt Borland, hold degrees in engineering. Newman got his Bachelor of Science in Vehicle Structural Engineeering from Purdue University, where he graduated in August of 2001.

Newman has already demonstrated that formal education can play an important role in his success as a NEXTEL Cup driver. Three full seasons into his promising career, Newman already has Darrell Waltrip's modern-era qualifying record of 59 poles in sight. And he also has his eye on the NEXTEL Cup championship.

STATS (SINCE 2000)

YEAR	STARTS	WINS	TOP 5	TOP 10	MONEY
2000	1	0	0	0	$37,825
2001	7	0	2	2	$465,276
2002	36	1	14	22	$5,346,651
2003	36	8	17	22	$6,100,877
2004	36	2	11	14	$5,152,666
CAREER	**116**	**11**	**44**	**60**	**$17,103,295**

12

Birthdate: December 8, 1977

Birthplace: South Bend, IN

Team: Penske Racing South

Sponsor: ALLTEL

Owner: Roger Penske

Crew Chief: Matt Borland

Car: Dodge

Ryan Newman focuses on the job at hand as he waits for the green flag.

Ricky RUDD

If any driver in the NEXTEL Cup garage could adopt Frank Sinatra's "My Way" as a theme song, Ricky Rudd would be the ideal candidate, now that Dave Marcis has retired.

Though he his driven for some of the most renowned owners in stock car racing—Junie Donlavey, Richard Childress, Bud Moore, Kenny Bernstein, Rick Hendrick and Robert Yates—Rudd has essentially done it "his way" ever since he first climbed behind the steering wheel of a Winston Cup stock car in 1975.

Driving the No. 10 Ford owned by Bill Champion, the 18-year-old Rudd qualified 26th at Rockingham and parlayed that middle-of-the-pack start into an 11th-place finish, 56 laps down to race winner Cale Yarborough. Though Rudd would compete in only eight Cup races over the next two years, his performance at Rockingham was a solid indication of great things to come.

From 1976 through 1978, Rudd drove cars owned by his father, Al Rudd Sr. With ten top-ten finishes in 25 races in 1977, he claimed the NEXTEL Cup Rookie of the Year title. Driving for Donlavey, his father, and Bill Gardner, respectively, in 1979, 1980 and 1981, Rudd failed to win a race, but he finished second three times and earned sixth place in the championship standings in Gardner's No. 88 DiGard car (a Buick, Oldsmobile or Chevrolet, depending on the race).

Rudd signed with the fledgling Childress organization in 1982, and a year later, the Chesapeake, Virginia, driver won his first race on June 5 on the 2.62-mile road course at Riverside (California) International Raceway.

Appropriately, Rudd would earn the reputation throughout his career as one of the top road-course racers on the NEXTEL Cup circuit.

Rudd won his second race later that year at Martinsville, the site of his eye-opening debut eight years earlier. His 1983 victories marked the beginning of a 16-year streak that would see Rudd win at least one race per season through 1998, his penultimate year as an owner/driver. Ironically, Rudd has never won more than two races in a single season in a 28-year career.

A remarkably consistent performer throughout his career, Rudd has finished in the top 10 in the championship standings 18 times. He came closest to winning the NEXTEL Cup title in 1991, when he finished second in the No. 5 Hendrick Chevy, 195 points behind series champion Dale Earnhardt.

Ten years later, in his second season with Yates after six years as an owner/driver, Rudd was eventual champion Jeff Gordon's closest pursuer until mechanical problems at the Brickyard and at Michigan dimmed his title hopes.

Signing on with Yates in 2000 energized a career that had spiraled into mediocrity under the pressure of running the team and driving the racecar at the same time. From a sixth-place finish in the points in 1996, Rudd had slipped to 17th in 1997, 22nd in 1998 and 31st in 1999—almost in inverse proportion to the escalating cost of keeping a competitive race team on the track.

Though he failed to win a race in his first season behind the wheel of Yates' powerful No. 28 Ford, Rudd improved to fifth in the championship standings. In his battle with Gordon in 2001, he returned to Victory Lane for the first time in 88 races—at Martinsville, no less—and followed that with a win at Richmond, where he played bumper tag with rookie Kevin Harvick, whom he passed for the lead with six laps remaining.

21

Birthdate: September 12, 1956

Birthplace: Chesapeake, VA

Team: Wood Brothers

Sponsor: Motorcraft

Owner: Eddie Wood, Glen Wood, Len Wood

Crew Chief: Michael McSwain

Car: Ford

Ricky Rudd shed the pressure of competing as an owner/driver when he took over the controls of Robert Yates' No. 28 Ford.

Ricky **RUDD**

Rudd began the 2002 campaign recuperating from surgery to repair a bulging disc in his lower back. He had woken up one morning during race week at Dover, Delaware, and noticed a pain he had never experienced before. It might have been an omen, for the 2002 season would be one of extreme turmoil within the Yates organization, and it would be Rudd's last with RYR.

In 2003 he signed with his fellow Virginians, the Wood Brothers, and suffered through an uneven year that brought four top fives and a 23rd-place finish in points. The 2004 season, however, brought some promising signs. Rudd won the pole for the first Talladega race. Reunited with crew chief Michael "Fatback" McSwain late in the year, Rudd qualified second for the fall Talladega race and finished second at Kansas City on successive weekends. Though early-season setbacks hurt him in points, Rudd had reason to look toward 2005 with an air of optimism.

Ricky Rudd's previous Ford is little more than a blur as it flashes past the grandstand.

STATS (SINCE 2000)

YEAR	STARTS	WINS	TOP 5	TOP 10	MONEY
2000	34	0	12	19	$2,914,970
2001	36	2	14	22	$4,878,027
2002	36	1	8	12	$4,444,614
2003	36	0	4	5	$3,240,614
2004	36	0	1	3	$3,697,099
CAREER	839	23	192	364	$35,912,550

Elliott SADLER

As long as Elliott Sadler has been racing, it is difficult to believe he just turned 29 in April of 2004.

The younger brother of veteran Busch Series driver Hermie Sadler, the Emporia, Virginia, native began his career in Go-Karts at age 7 and won more than 200 races before trying his hand in a stock car in 1993. South Boston (Va.) Speedway has proved a fertile training ground over the years, and Sadler was yet another beneficiary of the intense weekend competition there.

In 1995 he won 13 races and the track championship in late model stocks. He also got his first taste of competition in the Busch Series racing that year, when NASCAR's second-tier road show visited South Boston. By 1997, Sadler was a full-time competitor in the Busch Series, and he made the most of his opportunity—he won three races and finished fifth in the championship standings.

The 1998 season brought his debut in NEXTEL Cup. Driving a car owned by Gary Bechtel, Sadler qualified 31st for the May 24 Coca-Cola 600 at Charlotte and finished 42nd in his first appearance in NASCAR's top series. At the end of the season, Sadler began a long-term association with the vaunted Wood Brothers team when he competed in the Coca-Cola 200 exhibition race on the road course at Motegi, Japan; he started fourth and finished 20th.

Running a full schedule with the Wood Brothers in 1999, Sadler posted one top-10 and finished second to Tony Stewart in the battle for Rookie of the Year honors. But the promise of 1999 dissolved into disappointment in 2000, when Sadler failed to qualify for the first race at Talladega and failed to finish four other races. With one top-10 to his credit in 33 races, Sadler was 29th in points—and highly motivated to improve in 2001.

STATS (SINCE 2000)

YEAR	STARTS	WINS	TOP 5	TOP 10	MONEY
2000	33	0	0	1	$1,579,656
2001	36	1	2	2	$2,683,225
2002	36	0	2	7	$3,491,694
2003	36	0	2	9	$3,795,174
2004	36	2	8	14	$5,018,362
CAREER	**213**	**3**	**14**	**34**	**$18,202,657**

True enough, the 2001 season produced several milestones for Sadler and his team. After wrecking his primary car and staring 38th on a provisional, the young driver posted his first NEXTEL Cup victory in his 75th start, at Bristol on March 25. That was the Wood Brothers' first trip to Victory Lane since Morgan Shepherd won at Atlanta on March 20, 1993. Sadler finished a career-best 20th in points in 2001 and matched his best-ever qualifying effort on back-to-back weekends at Michigan and Bristol. When Dale Earnhardt Jr. took the checkered flag at the end of the emotionally-charged Pepsi 400 at Daytona in July, Sadler crossed the finish line third.

The most significant boost to Sadler's career came in 2003, when Robert Yates hired him to drive the No. 38 M&M's Ford. After a year of acclimation to the Yates machines and a 22nd-place finish in points, Sadler showed dramatic improvement in 2004. From the 19th starting position at Texas Motor Speedway, Sadler posted the second victory of his career. He backed that up with a win at the 2-mile oval in Fontana, California. Those two victories propelled Sadler into the Chase for the NEXTEL Cup, and he earned a spot on stage for the awards banquet in December with a ninth-place finish in points, 11 places better than his previous best result. Obviously, if Sadler can continues to take steps of that magnitude, a title could come his way in the near future.

Sadler showed he meant business in 2004 with his M&M's Ford

38

Birthdate: April 30, 1975

Birthplace: Emporia, VA

Team: Robert Yates Racing

Sponsor: M&M's

Owner: Robert Yates

Crew Chief: Todd Parrott

Car: Ford

Tony **STEWART**

When tempestuous Tony Stewart arrived on the NEXTEL Cup scene with all the fanfare that usually accompanies a coronation, he arrived with an abundance of self-confidence—and a petulant attitude to go with it.

But his no-holds-barred talk and occasional explosions of temper quickly took a back seat to one of the most remarkable rookie seasons in NEXTEL Cup history. It's not enough to note that Stewart won the Rookie of the Year title in a landslide. For one thing, with victories at Richmond, Phoenix and Homestead in a stunning second-half of the 1999 season, the Rushville (Indiana) Rocket became the first driver ever to win three races during his rookie campaign.

With an astounding 13 top-five finishes and 21 top-10s, he finished fourth in the final points standings, proving that he had made the difficult transition from open-wheeled cars to stock cars without missing a beat. Three years later, Stewart was sitting at the head table at the Waldorf-Astoria in New York as champion of NASCAR's elite series.

Stewart's racing resume dates to 1983, when at age 12 he won the International Karting Foundation Grand National championship. He progress through the ranks was meteoric. In 1993 he won his first USAC Midget feature in Terre Haute, Indiana. By the time the 1995 season ended, he was national champion in USAC's Midget, Sprint and Silver Crown series; no driver before him had ever won the title in all three divisions in the same season.

In 1996 Stewart was Rookie of the Year for the Indianapolis 500, where he won the pole and led the first 44 laps. In 1997 he was Indy Racing League champion.

As Stewart prepared for his eventual move to NEXTEL Cup, he split time between the Busch Series and the Indy Racing League. Though he was a full-time NEXTEL Cup driver in 1999, he nevertheless ran the Indianapolis 500 and NASCAR's Coca-Cola 600 on the same day (May 30), completing 1,090 of a possible 1,100 miles in the two races. After finishing ninth at Indy, Stewart jetted to Charlotte, where he battled to a fourth-place result.

The 2000 season brought a series-best six victories—at both Dover races, Michigan, New Hampshire, Martinsville and Homestead—and solidified Stewart's reputation as perhaps the best "flat-track" driver in the NEXTEL Cup Series. Despite his prolific number of wins, however, Stewart slipped to sixth in points, a result directly attributable to his failure to finish five races.

A late-season surge in 2001 gave Stewart his best points finish to that point, second to champion Jeff Gordon. Stewart added three more victories to his growing list of accomplishments—on the road course at Sears Point (Sonoma, California), at Richmond and at Bristol. Astoundingly, he actually *improved* on his 1999 "daily double" at Indianapolis and Charlotte when he finished sixth in the Indy 500 and third in the Coca-Cola 600, completing all 1,100 miles.

As the 2002 season approached, the brash 30-year-old with a penchant for bowling, cheeseburgers and video games made a conscious effort to present a kinder, gentler image—thanks perhaps to the influence of car owner Joe Gibbs, the former Washington Redskins coach whose strait-laced demeanor has provided a sharp contrast to his impetuous driver's lack of restraint.

Stewart also announced his intention to try to eliminate outside distractions during the 2002 season, the implication being that if a reporter doesn't shove a tape recorder under his nose as soon as he climbs out of his car, Stewart won't grab the offending machine and throw it beneath a nearby transporter (as he once did). "If it doesn't make the racecar go faster or doesn't promote Home Depot (his sponsor), I'm

20

Birthdate: May 20, 1971

Birthplace: Rushville, IN

Team: Joe Gibbs Racing

Sponsor: Home Depot

Owner: Joe Gibbs

Crew Chief: Greg Zipadelli

Car: Chevrolet

Everything about Tony Stewart is explosive—from his talent to his temperament.

not doing it," he said. "I'm not messing with it. I'm not messing with the outside distractions…

"Being volatile doesn't make you a good race driver. Winning races makes you a good racecar driver. The distractions outside the car are what make me volatile, so we're eliminating the distractions. I probably won't be volatile this year."

Distracted or not, tempestuous or not, Stewart won

> # Being volatile doesn't make you a good race driver. Winning races makes you a good race car driver.

three times in 2002 and cruised to the NEXTEL Cup title. His championship run included 15 top-five finishes in 36 points races.

In 2003, Stewart won twice but slipped to seventh in points, his worst career finish. The 2004 season brought two more victories and a sixth-place finish in the Chase for the NEXTEL Cup. Remarkably, in six seasons of NEXTEL Cup racing, Stewart has finished no worse than seventh in the final standings. But for the mercurial driver, anything less than a championship is unacceptable.

Tony Stewart visited Victory Lane three times in his rookie year.

STATS (SINCE 2000)

YEAR	STARTS	WINS	TOP 5	TOP 10	MONEY
2000	34	6	12	23	$3,642,348
2001	36	3	15	22	$4,941,463
2002	36	3	15	21	$9,163,761
2003	36	2	12	18	$6,136,633
2004	36	2	10	19	$6,161,710
CAREER	**212**	**19**	**76**	**124**	**$33,236,064**

Brian VICKERS

When Brian Vickers learns to finish as proficiently as he starts, he'll be a major force in NEXTEL Cup racing.

Already a key player in the Hendrick Motorsports youth movement, Vickers replaced Joe Nemechek in the No. 25 Chevrolet late in the 2003 season. At the same time, Vickers was embroiled in the most hotly contested championship battle in Busch Series history.

Vickers was barely 20 years old when he secured the Busch title with an 11th-place finish at Homestead-Miami Speedway, but by then, the youngest champion in Busch Series history had already established himself as a formidable qualifier in NEXTEL Cup.

In his second race in NASCAR's premier division, at Atlanta, Vickers started fourth. In each of the following two weeks, at Phoenix and Rockingham, he qualified second. And the day before he was to race for the Busch title at Homestead, he grabbed the third starting position for the final NEXTEL Cup race of the season.

The quality of Vickers' NEXTEL Cup finishes wasn't equal to the strength of his starts. Nor did he match his efforts in the Busch Series, where he won three times and finished second twice in claiming the title for the late Ricky Hendrick, his friend and car owner.

Vickers' best result in limited NEXTEL Cup action in 2003 was a 13th at Phoenix. As the 2004 season unfolded, the young driver suffered from the same chronic problem: start up front, finish in the back.

Vickers won two poles in his rookie season, at Richmond and California. On three other occasions, at Atlanta, Michigan and Pocono, he started on the outside of the front row. By the season's midpoint, Vickers had already enjoyed a stretch of five straight top-five starts. The problem was, those outstanding two-lap qualifying efforts weren't translating into sustained success during the races.

Vickers led 32 laps from the pole at Richmond but slipped to eighth by the end of the race. A ninth at Michigan and a ninth in the Pepsi 400 at Daytona in July were his only other top 10s before the October Atlanta race, which took place a week after a plane crash claimed the life of Ricky Hendrick and nine others. It was Hendrick's retirement from driving (in the aftermath of injuries sustained on the track) that had given Vickers the opportunity to drive the No. 5 Hendrick Chevy in the Busch Series.

Hendrick was on the way to Martinsville, Virginia, to serve as spotter for the No. 25 NEXTEL Cup team when the Hendrick plane crashed in the fog. The tragedy clearly had a devastating effect on Vickers, but he rallied a week later with the seventh-place finish at Atlanta, as teammate Jimmie Johnson won the race.

There's no doubt that Vickers is quick, but before he becomes a frontrunner in NEXTEL Cup, he must learn to do more than run a couple of hot laps during qualifying. As experience begins to temper his aggressive style, Vickers could become one of the top drivers in the sport.

STATS (SINCE 2000)

YEAR	STARTS	WINS	TOP 5	TOP 10	MONEY
2000	did not compete				
2001	did not compete				
2002	did not compete				
2003	5	0	0	0	$263,484
2004	36	0	0	4	$3,044,898
CAREER	**41**	**0**	**0**	**4**	**$3,308,382**

25

Birthdate: October 29, 1983

Birthplace: Thomasville, NC

Team: Hendrick Motorsports

Sponsor: GMAC Financial Services

Owner: Rick Hendrick

Crew Chief: Lance McGrew

Car: Chevrolet

Back in Black: Brian Vickers is definitely a driver to watch for future NEXTEL Cup championships.

Rusty WALLACE

In Winston Cup racing, "50" is the magic number. It's the passkey to the elite inner circle of stock car racing legends, a one-way ticket to the Hall of Fame.

Drivers with 50 or more career victories occupy a special place in NEXTEL Cup lore, because so few among the hundreds who have attempted to win even one race have reached that lofty number.

In more than 50 years of NASCAR racing, only 11 men have won 50 or more times. Of the active drivers on the NEXTEL Cup circuit, only two have reached that milestone. One is four-time series champion Jeff Gordon, who stood seventh on the all-time list with 69 victories through October of 2004

The other is veteran Rusty Wallace, the garrulous short-track specialist who at the pinnacle of his proficiency won 10 races in 1993. Through October of 2004, Wallace had 55 victories to his credit—tied with Lee Petty for eighth on the career list and immediately ahead of such luminaries as Ned Jarrett and Junior Johnson, who posted 50 wins each.

The son of a racing father, Wallace learned his craft at Lakehill Speedway in Valley Park, Missouri, where he won more than 200 stock car features between 1974 and 1978. In 1979 he joined the USAC stock car series and claimed the Rookie of the Year title with five victories.

In 1980, Wallace made his debut in NEXTEL Cup in a car owned by Roger Penske. He finished second to 1980 series champion Dale Earnhardt on March 16 at Atlanta. Wallace also raced for Penske in the National 500 at Charlotte that year, starting 15th and finishing 14th. Eleven years would pass before Wallace would drive for Penske in the NEXTEL Cup Series again.

After winning the American Speed Association championship in 1983, Wallace made his formal graduation to NEXTEL Cup in 1984, driving a full schedule in Cliff Stewart's No. 88 Pontiac. After a second winless season in 1985, Wallace accepted a ride from owner Raymond Beadle in the No. 27 Blue Max Racing Pontiac.

It was on April 6, 1986 that Wallace recorded his first career victory at Bristol and began to establish his reputation as a master of the short tracks. He won again on September 21 at Martinsville.

From 1986 on, Wallace won at least one event per year for 16 straight years (until a winless 2002 campaign broke the streak). In 1988, still driving for Beadle, he finished second to Bill Elliott in one of the closest championship races in NEXTEL Cup history; Wallace ended the season 24 points behind Awesome Bill.

In 1989, Wallace edged Dale Earnhardt for his only series title by an even closer margin—12 points. In winning six races during his championship run, Wallace became the eighth driver in NEXTEL Cup history to exceed $5 million in career prize money—a total that today represents a single season for a top driver.

The championship battle came down to the season's final race at Atlanta, where Wallace had to finish no more than 18 places behind Earnhardt to clinch the title. Earnhardt won the race itself—an event clouded by the death of driver Grant Adcox after a fiery crash on Lap 202—but Wallace rallied to finish 15th and secured the championship.

Wallace parted with Beadle after a sixth-place finish in points in 1990 and began an association with Penske that has lasted more than a decade. He was second in points in 1993, 80 behind Earnhardt, despite his ten victories. In 1994, Wallace added eight more wins to his side of the ledger. After winning two events in 1995 and five in 1996, Wallace posted one victory per year in 1997, 1998 and 1999

Rusty Wallace is one of two active drivers to have reached the 50-win milestone

before returning to form and winning four times in 2000.

Lean times returned in 2001, the same year Wallace reached his 45th birthday, though he won his only race of the year at California Speedway, a track built by and owned by Penske.

Missing from Wallace's list of accomplishments is a victory at either of the restrictor-plate superspeedways—Daytona or Talladega—though Wallace has provided his share of highlights at each of the facilities.

His spectacular barrel rolls past the start/finish line at Talladega in May of 1993 helped speed the introduction of

> # I've won just about everywhere except Daytona.

a new safety feature mandated by NASCAR—roof flaps designed to prevent cars from becoming airborne in a high-speed crash.

Though Wallace has a championship to his credit, he believes a victory in the Daytona 500 would be a capstone to his career. "Yes, absolutely, I think so," Wallace says. "I've won just about everywhere except Daytona and should have won Daytona three or four times but didn't do it."

During the 2004 season, Wallace announced that the 2005 campaign would be his last in NEXTEL Cup racing. With or without a Daytona 500 win, Wallace will retire as one of the all-time greats of the sport.

The Miller Lite Ford is always a threat to win.

STATS (SINCE 2000)

YEAR	STARTS	WINS	TOP 5	TOP 10	MONEY
2000	34	4	12	20	$3,621,468
2001	36	1	8	14	$4,788,652
2002	36	0	7	17	$4,785,134
2003	36	0	2	12	$4,246,547
2004	36	1	3	11	$4,447,302
CAREER	670	55	194	332	$43,136,702